Y0-ATD-909

Library of
Davidson College

Charity
  in the Novels
of Galdós

Charity
in the Novels
of Galdós

Arnold M. Penuel

University of Georgia Press, Athens

For Patty

Library of Congress Catalog Card Number: 77–188570
International Standard Book Number: 0–8203–0291–0

The University of Georgia Press, Athens 30601

Copyright © 1972 by the University of Georgia Press
All rights reserved.

Printed in the United States of America

863

P4 381xpe

75-7197

Contents

Preface

IN THIS STUDY I examine the theme of charity of love in Galdós's *Novelas de la primera época* and *Novelas españolas contemporáneas*. Because of their primarily historical content I have excluded the *Episodios nacionales*.

It should be made clear from the outset that the use of the word "charity" in the title of the study is the result of a compromise. "Love" would have been a more suitable choice except for two considerations: (1) there is no intention to study sexual love per se in the novels and (2) "love" does not specifically include the meaning of "organized philanthropy" which does form a part of the study. "Charity," although archaic, was selected because, while it excludes the idea of sexual love, it includes the other meanings of "love" and the idea of organized philanthropy. While there is no intention to analyze frustrated sexual love here, it may figure in the discussion when it is an element of the dynamics of other types of love or of hatred. To assure clarity with respect to the precise purview of the study, "charity" is considered to include the following meanings: (1) the love of man for God and for his fellow men in Christianity; (2) the feeling of benevolence and tolerance toward others; (3) acts of compassion or kindness toward others; (4) the giving of money, advice, and other help to those who are in need; (5) institutional help for those in need; (6) self-sacrifice; (7) self-love and self-hatred. Cruelty and intolerance are included where the absence of charity per se is thematically focal. The category of friendship is subsumed under the various aspects of charity.

Because of Galdós's genial ability to derive as many uses as possible from a given situation involving charity I have had to make a judgment as to the primary significance of any given instance of charity. Accordingly many situations involving charity are discussed primarily from one perspective. The manifold implications of other instances have required that they be treated from diverse points of view.

I wish to express my deep appreciation to Professor W. H. Shoemaker who further stimulated my interest in Galdós and provided me with many tools for understanding him. I am also greatly indebted to Professor Robert W. Linker for his valuable suggestions and criticisms, to Professor Brian Dutton for his encouragement, and to the staff of the University of Georgia Press who aided in the preparation of the manuscript.

Introduction

TO UNDERSTAND CHARITY in the Spain of the latter half of the nineteenth century, it is helpful to know something about religion and public beneficence as practiced then. According to the noted historian Antonio Ramos-Oliveira, the Church in Spain during this period was often found in direct contradiction to the teachings of Christ on charity: "El clero provinciano y aldeano allanaba moradas, se apoderaba de de los muertos, secuestraba a menores y los metía en los conventos sin la acquiescencia paterna; injuriaba al disidente o arruinaba al heterodoxo."[1]

The strongest and most organized opposition to this state of affairs came from the Krausists.[2] Without denying religion, the Krausists laid stress on a rationalistic humanitarian approach to the solution of mankind's problems. For the Krausists, Christianity was only a stage in the religious evolution of man. The final goal was a religion without dogmas, miracles, and divine revelation; reason and the conscience were to be the arbiters of individual conduct.[3] Religious dogma and party spirit were denounced as socially divisive and productive of intolerance. Harking back to the teachings of Christ, the Krausists saw charity as the cure for individual and social evils: "Et le meilleur remède aux maux dont nous souffrons et dont la vie de Dieu nous donne le parfait exemplaire et qui s'appelle la Charité."[4] The very necessity the Krausists felt of insisting upon charity as the basis of human relations, as if it were something new, implied their conviction that the Church in Spain had deviated from the practice of this fundamental Christian virtue.

The introduction into Spain in the 1850s of this liberal philosophy was bitterly opposed by the Neo-Catholics, whose principal organ of propaganda was the newspaper *El Pensamiento Español.* The controversy continued through the 1850s and 1860s until the Revolution of 1868 when the new government's attempt to establish religious freedom aroused, in the words of the historian Martin Hume, "all the blind bigotry of ancient Spain."[5] And as Stephen Scatori[6] has pointed out, it is a problem with which nearly all Spanish intellectuals have been grappling from that day until the present. As might well be expected, the principal Spanish novelists of the latter half of the century could hardly avoid reflecting the religious polemic in their novels.

Although records of public beneficence in Spain date back to the Visigothic occupation of the peninsula, its organization in the latter half of the nineteenth century was based largely on laws of 1849 and 1852. An attempt was made in this legislation to reconcile public and private beneficence. A royal decree in 1875 further defined the boundaries between the two sectors of beneficence, confirming at the same time the state's right of inspection over all charitable institutions. Provision was made for a *Junta Municipal de Beneficencia* in each municipal government under the jurisdiction of the Department of the Interior (Gobernación). Its function was to distribute alms to the needy and provide them with free medical care in their homes.[7]

Studies made of both public and private charity during the period permit at least three broad generalizations: poverty was widespread, charity was too indiscriminately and poorly administered to serve as more than a means of stopgap relief, the particular organization of charity tended to foster professional mendicancy. Needless to say, a strong implication of extensive social injustice underlies these generalizations. Statistics for the year 1887 provided by R. W. Turner, the American consul in Cadiz, reveal both the extent of the pauperism in Spain as well as one of its principal causes: of a total population of 16,654,345, charitable institutions housed 500,000 individuals. Now the root of the problem: only 4,071,823 of the total population could read and write; 11,978,168 could do neither; and 5,376 were unclassified.[8] The consul cites the failure of public charity to get to the root of the problem of poverty:

Personal study of the question forces me to recognize the Spanish people as ranking among the most charitable of the world, but their charities, as a rule, are so badly organized, or better said, so unorganized, that they have no effect in building into self-dependency the dependent classes of society. . . . Their [charities] distribution is indiscriminate and does not have as an object anything more serious than temporary relief.[9]

Turner observes that as a consequence of the lackadaisical attitude of municipal and government authorities toward the administration of charity, begging acquired the status of a profession:

No efforts are being made for the suppression or punishment of begging, hence it has taken to itself the dignity of a profession, and every village, town, and city swarms with mendicants. Beggars are licensed by city councils, said license being restricted to the poor that are natives of the city's jurisdiction, for instance, the poor of Cadiz are not entitled to a license to beg in Jerez, and vice versa.[10]

In the same consular reports the American consul in Malaga, T. W. Newson, comes to essentially the same conclusions with respect to the professionalism of the beggars in Spain.[11] Lest the reader be left with an entirely negative picture of public charity in Spain, Turner does praise as the best charity systems the orphan asylums, industrial training schools for the young, asylums for the aged, and hospitals for the sick and handicapped.[12]

Perhaps the most frequently commented, yet least studied aspect of the novels of the nineteenth century Spanish novelist, Benito Pérez Galdós (1843-1920), is the theme of love or charity. Numerous critics have seen charity as the heart of Galdós's ethical beliefs. Marcelino Menéndez y Pelayo asserts that the novels of Galdós "tienen, sobre todo, un hondo sentido de caridad humana, una simpatía universal por los débiles, por los afligidos y menesterosos, por los niños abandonados, por las víctimas de la ignorancia y del vicio, y hasta por los cesantes y los llamados cursis."[13] Echoing the beautiful New Testament passage on charity, Hayward Keniston says this: "Freedom, justice, love,—these are his themes and the greatest of these is love. Again and again in his noblest works he tells the story of triumphant love, a love that is greater than self, greater than honor, greater than death."[14] L. B. Walton affirms that "Galdós accepts life unquestioningly; and to all its problems he finds an answer in the exercise of charity. Charity, to him, is the central fact of human existence."[15] César Barja also sees love as the most salient feature of Galdós's novels: "Lo que en la totalidad de la obra galdosiana resplandece es un supremo idealismo amoroso, una piedad y una compasión grandes por el dolor ajeno."[16] For Hilario Sáenz charity is the essence of religion from the viewpoint of the novelist: "Cree Galdós que la esencia de la religión es la caridad, el amor a las criaturas. Dios se nos manifiesta en nuestras relaciones humanas de amor y caridad."[17] Christian love as the only solution to Spain's most difficult problems is considered by Angel del Río as "una de las obsesiones de Galdós que da a toda su obra."[18] The observation which Sherman Eoff makes on the subject is succinct: "The novelist's most outstanding ideal is harmonious progress through the medium of love."[19] The reader interested in additional critical comments on the importance of the theme of charity in Galdós's novels will not have to search far, since his critics have been generous in making such observations.[20]

Notes

[1] *Historia de España* (1952), 2: 423–424.

[2] Krausism had its origin in Spain with the promulgation by Julián Sanz del Río (1814–1869) of the ideas of a minor German philosopher, Karl Friedrich Krause (1781–1832). Under the leadership of Sanz del Río, the Krausists had their greatest influence in Spain from 1857 to 1869, although another Krausist, Francisco Giner de los Ríos (1839–1915), founder of the *Institución Libre de Enseñanza* (1876), continued to exert a strong influence on Spanish intellectual life in the last quarter of the century.

[3] A thorough discussion of Krausism is found in Juan López-Morillas, *El krausismo español* (1956).

[4] Pierre Jobit, *Les educateurs de L'Espagne contemporaine* (1936), p. 93.

[5] *Modern Spain,* 3rd ed. (1923), p. 476.

[6] *La idea religiosa en la obra de Benito Pérez Galdós* (1926), p. 18.

[7] The discussion of the legislative aspects of beneficence is based on "Beneficencia," *Enciclopedia Universal Ilustrada.*

[8] United States Foreign Commerce Bureau, "Vagrancy and Public Charities in Foreign Countries," *Special Consular Reports,* 9 (1893): 370. Hume cites these statistics with regard to the percentage of the population able to write: 1860, 19.97 percent; 1885, 28 percent (p. 546).

[9] *Special Consular Reports,* p. 369.

[10] Ibid.

[11] Ibid.

[12] Ibid.

[13] *Estudios de crítica literaria* (1908), p. 119. The study on Galdós was given as a speech in 1897 on the occasion of Galdós's entrance into the *Real Academia Española.*

[14] "Galdós, Interpreter of Life," *Hispania,* 3 (1920): 206.

[15] *Pérez Galdós and the Spanish Novel of the Nineteenth Century* (1927), p. 234.

[16] *Libros y autores modernos* (1933), p. 238.

[17] "Ideario galdosiano," *Hispania,* 28 (1945): 368.

[18] *Estudios galdosianos* (1953), p. 33.

[19] *The Novels of Pérez Galdós: The Concept of Life as Dynamic Process* (1954), p. 139.

[20] For additional representative examples, see Salvador de Madariaga, *The Genius of Spain* (1923), pp. 62-63; Hubert Hüsges, *Der Schriftsteller Benito Pérez Galdós (1843-1920) als Vorkämpfer des Liberalismus in Spanien* (1928), p. 27; F. M. Kercheville, "Galdós and the New Humanism," *MLS,* 16 (1931): 480–481; Federico de Onís, "El españolismo de Galdós," *Ensayos sobre el sentido de la cultura española* (1932), p. 116; W. H. Shoemaker, "Preliminary Study" to *Crónica de la Quincena* by Benito Pérez Galdós (1948), pp. 37–38; Ramón Pérez de Ayala, *Divagaciones literarias,* (1958), pp. 127–128. Gilberto Paolini, *An Aspect of the Spiritualistic Naturalism in the Novels of B. P. Galdós: Charity* (1969). In his study of Galdós's novels Paolini deals with charity as a theological virtue, concluding that Galdós's recognition of the presence of a "charitable embryo in each person is tantamount to destroying the hypothesis that certain of his novels belong to French naturalism" (p. 10). Paolini's study deals with both true and false charity.

I   Psychological Aspects of Charity

A MEANINGFUL MEASURE of the breadth of Galdós's approach to human affairs requires a knowledge of individual novels such as *Fortunata y Jacinta* (1886–1887), where one finds representatives of varied social classes, professions, and points of view interacting. A successful horizontal presentation of human affairs is one facet of Galdós's genius; another facet is his perspicuity in exploiting the vertical or psychological dimensions of human conduct. One manifestation of his ability to portray his characters in depth is his accurate pre-Freudian use of the subconscious in the presentation of abnormal characters. Studies have been made by F. M. Kercheville and L. W. Eliot,[1] John Iwanik,[2] Ricardo Gullón,[3] and Joseph Schraibman,[4] of the subconscious in Galdós's portrayal of abnormal characters. What is often overlooked is his constant recourse to sound psychological principles, sometimes involving the concept of the subconscious, sometimes not, in the presentation of many characters who are considered normal by most critics.

Before examining charity in Galdós's novels from the psychological perspective, I wish to consider briefly some of his basic assumptions with respect to psychology. Of utmost importance is his conception of personality. In "La mujer del filósofo," he has stated a strong belief in innate qualities developed by education: "Dos causas determinan principalmente el carácter de las personas: las cualidades innatas o las que nacen y se desarrollan en la naturaleza a consecuencia de la educación y del trato" (VI, 1650).[5]

Since no systematic study has been made of the conception of personality in Galdós's novels, what follows must be considered a hypothesis.[6] The conception of personality is not

1

only indispensable in understanding Galdós's psychology of love but in turn a study of this psychology confirms that the hypothesis is a fruitful one. His treatment of characters throughout the novels confirms his belief in a hard inner core of the personality which is a constitutional predisposition and is resistant to change. The presence of this inner core, which might be called the self, is usually revealed in the characters by its very resistance to change; the borders of the self are defined by a reaction to their being violated by elements foreign to the essential nature of the self. This self is like a balloon which, when it is depressed in one area, protrudes in another, thereby preserving its unity, though in a distorted fashion. This phenomenon is often demonstrated in Galdós's characters. It is dramatic in obviously abnormal characters such as Paulita Porreño, Maximiliano Rubín, Abelarda Villaamil, Angel Guerra, and Rafael del Aguila, who all distort their inner self in one way or another, only to learn at last that they have been false to their innermost nature. From the viewpoint of psychoanalysis these characters have repressed instinctual urges because of internalized demands made upon them by some other person or by society in general. Their externally erratic acts reveal the difficulty they have in repressing their true nature. In all of these characters the real self finally asserts itself by breaking through the subconscious repression and releasing itself. What is true of abnormal characters holds true in more subtle ways with supposedly normal characters.

Another aspect of Galdós's conception of the self is that, although it is unique in each individual, there are areas in which all human beings are alike.[7] The inability of Angel in *Angel Guerra* (1890–1891) to renounce passionate love, while Leré makes such a sacrifice, illustrates the uniqueness of each self. The need of every human being to love and be loved is one of the greatest areas in which all human beings coincide, according to Galdós's conception of personality hypothesized here.

Galdós's psychology of love is inextricably bound up with his conception of personality. Love is an essential ingredient in the psychological life of each and every individual. There are individual differences in both the ability to love and the ability to attract love, but being the recipient of love, as well as hate, invariably has a psychological impact on Galdós's characters. Psychological effects are likewise discernible in the characters who love or refuse to love.

With respect to his psychology of love, almost no discernible change or pattern of evolution has been detected which might distinguish Galdós's earlier novels from those of his artistic maturity. Nevertheless, while overt physical acts of aggression engendered by hatred occur in nearly all of the novels, in the *Novelas de la primera época* (1867–1878) there are no instances of hatred brought about by prolonged frustration or psychological aggression as demonstrated in the cases of Francisco Torquemada in the Torquemada series (1889–1895) and Aberlarda Villaamil in *Miau* (1888).

The Dynamics of Love and Hate

In Galdós's view, what are the psychological conditions which produce love or hate, in an individual? His answer to this question is essentially that love begets love and hate begets hate. In *La Fontana de Oro* (1867–1868) this idea is clearly demonstrated in the change of character in the *beata* doña Paulita Porreño, and in her comments on this change. She is one of the three devout Porreño women who have taken in the orphan Clara Chacón, ostensibly out of charity. In reality their protection of Clara permits them to treat her cruelly on the pretext that their stifling moral exhortations and censure are for her own good. A change occurs in doña Paulita, however, when she gradually, perhaps subconsciously at first, falls in love with Lázaro Orejón, a suitor and relative of Clara, who visits her frequently. Doña Paulita's love of Lázaro develops to the point that she confesses her love to him and proposes that they flee together.

What is more to the point here is what happens to the personality of doña Paulita under the influence of love and the anticipation of being loved. She begins to be bored with her usual devout reading, is less severe with Clara and Lázaro's peccadilloes, and is even amenable to the orphan's suggestion that they take walks in the fresh air (IV, 105, 108, 110). In short, she becomes more expansive and generous.

She herself makes what appears to be a casual remark, but is really an explanation of her own past cruelty and that of the other two *beatas,* as well as an insight into the reasons for her new expansiveness: "Y ¿Cómo quieren que sea buena una persona que no es amada?—dijo con admirable misticismo la dama—. Cuando un ser recibe ingratitudes y desprecios, sus sentimientos se agrian, se esteriliza la fuente del bien y del amor que hay en todo pecho humano. Cuando un ser no es amado, ha de ser malo por precisión" (IV, 127-128).[8]

The same psychological dynamics operate in *Doña Perfecta* (1876) in the hatred that Pepe Rey, a young engineer, develops toward his aunt, doña Perfecta Polentinos and toward Orbajosans in general. Pepe is warmly welcomed by doña Perfecta upon his arrival in the small town of Orbajosa, where he has come with the purpose of meeting and marrying his aunt's daughter, Rosario. The marriage has been arranged by doña Perfecta and Pepe's father before his arrival, with the consent, of course, of the two young persons involved. The initial affection with which doña Perfecta treats her nephew soon vanishes when, through skillful baiting by the village priest don Inocencio, the liberal but religious Pepe is made to appear as a malicious atheist who is against every religious principle held sacred by the fanatical aunt. Doña Perfecta's fanaticism leads her to oppose the marriage and to use a series of cruel, surreptitious stratagems to separate Pepe from Rosario and drive him out of Orbajosa. In addition, Pepe is plagued by a series of lawsuits initiated by Licurgo, a friend of doña Perfecta's, who hopes to acquire land owned by the engineer.

As Pepe begins to feel the effect of all these frustrations and hatred, the author describes his need for love: "Amor, amistad, aire sano para la respiración moral, luz para el alma, simpatía, fácil comercio de ideas y de sensaciones era lo que necesitaba de una manera imperiosa" (IV, 442). Speaking to doña Perfecta, Pepe reveals how hate has affected him: "Era razonable, y soy un bruto; era respetuoso, y soy insolente; era culto y me encuentro salvaje. Usted me ha traído a este extremo, irritándome y apartándome del camino del bien, por donde iba" (IV, 466).[9]

In a more ambivalent form, doña Perfecta's frustration of

4

Rosario's love for Pepe engenders a feeling of hatred in her toward her mother. Rosario's hatred is ambivalent because she feels it is her duty to love her mother. As she reveals in a spontaneous outburst while praying, however, her whole emotional attitude is one of hatred: "¡Señor, ¡que aborrezco a mi madre!"[10] The final outcome of doña Perfecta's fanatical hatred is the death of Pepe and the insanity of Rosario.

Fortunata y Jacinta (1886–1887) discloses another interesting case of hatred, this time subconscious, induced by accumulated frustrations. For a while the scrawny, sickly Maximiliano Rubín is able to repress his subconscious hatred of his wife, Fortunata, who after intermittent periods of infidelity to him, at last makes a final separation in order to prepare for the birth of her child by her lover, Juanito Santa Cruz. During this separation, Maxi tries to convince his aunt, with whom he lives, that he has completely divested himself of any hatred toward his estranged wife: "Tía de mi alma, a fuerza de pensar y padecer, he llegado a desprenderme de todas las pasiones y a no sentir en mí ni odio ni venganza" (v, 359). In spite of Maxi's self-proclaimed detachment, he is able, through a series of shrewd observations and deductions based on a subconscious desire for vengeance, to find the living quarters of his wife. His self-deception is only partial since he does consider killing Fortunata, but he wants to consider himself an impartial benefactor of his wife, according to the dictates of logic and reason, so he deceives himself into thinking that he is performing a Christian duty when he visits her to teach her a lesson. Maxi's thoughts are revealed in an interior monologue: "Si la mato no hay lección. La enseñanza es más cristiana que la muerte, quizá más cruel, y de seguro más lógica. . . . Que viva para que padezca y padeciendo aprenda" (v, 497). Segismundo Ballester, a friend of both Fortunata and Maxi, only sees the surface, and attempts to relieve Fortunata's fears of her husband: "Si está muy razonable y más tranquilo que nunca. Todas sus ideas son ideas de benevolencia y tolerancia" (v, 503). Maxi tells Fortunata that he comes to offer her his compassion and do her a great favor by teaching her a lesson (v, 507). He affirms his compassionate detachment when he speaks of "esta elevación con que yo miro las cosas"

5

(v, 508). Then comes the cruel lesson: with impassive coldness, Maxi tells Fortunata that Juanito, whom she still loves,
and her best friend, Aurora Samaniego, are lovers (v, 510).
In a jealous rage, Fortunata rises from the bed, leaving her
newly born son alone, and goes to Aurora's place of work,
where she assaults her former friend so furiously as to bring
on the internal hemorrhaging that causes her own death
later.

Maxi visits Fortunata again the night after the attack to
tell her with cold impassivity that what she has done to
Aurora will have the effect of drawing Juanito closer to his
new beloved. Maxi again lays stress on the benefits that
Fortunata hopefully will reap from this lesson. The author
comments that "la joven lloraba con angustia, y él no parecía
tenerle compasión" (v, 524). Under the guise of teaching his
wife a lesson, Maxi has, by a repression of his subconscious
sadism, and a rationalization of his cruelty as a Christian
virtue, managed to wreak vengeance on his wife. Undeniable
proof of his subconscious hatred is forthcoming when Fortunata, enraged at the suggestion that Aurora will be favored
by her attack, effectively strips away all of Maxi's rationaliza-
tions in an effort to incite him to kill Aurora and Juanito.
Fortunata shames him for his lack of honor in not having
revenged himself on Juanito and promises to love him and
be a model wife if he will commit this act. His defense
mechanisms dissolved, his anticipation of Fortunata's love
aroused, his hatred of Juanito in the open again, Maxi
rushes out of the room with money that Fortunata has
given him to buy a gun.[11] In laying bare Maxi's rationaliza-
tions, Fortunata intuitively senses his fear of Juanito, who
had beaten him up once; she thereby brings to his conscious-
ness again his suppressed hatred of her former lover.

The death of Francisco Torquemada begins in the second
novel of the Torquemada series, *Torquemada en la cruz*
(1893) and is consummated in *Torquemada y San Pedro*
(1895), the last novel of the series. His death is long in
coming about because it is purely spiritual in its initial and
intermediate stages; in these stages, Torquemada, although
he flourishes materially, loses that part of his inner self that
makes him unique as a human being. He is spiritually can-

nibalized by his sister-in-law, Cruz del Aguila. His physical death in the last novel is paradoxically a healthy psychosomatic reaction to the loss of his soul. As strange as it may seem, the death of the prosperous former usurer illustrates the biblical assertion that no man lives by bread alone. Every man has a unique human essence which must find expression, and must be respected if life is to have any meaning for him.

From the beginning of Torquemada's marriage with Fidela, Cruz uses him as a means to restore the del Aguila family to its former rank in society.[12] At first, Torquemada shows little objection to Cruz's little hints that he improve his dress, speech, and manners, since he is still awed by his marriage into the aristocracy and the prospect of the prestige to accrue therefrom (v, 961).

In *Torquemada en el purgatorio* (1894), Cruz becomes more arrogant; the hints evolve into commands, although Cruz always appears to have persuaded the miserly Torquemada that in his new position of rank and increased wealth, decorum requires that he make certain changes and acquisitions, which he really feels are useless luxuries.[13] In the second and third novels, Torquemada's voiced opposition to Cruz's "proposals" is ineffectual from the standpoint of having his way, but his hyperbolical language does produce an effective humor.

From the beginning of *Torquemada y San Pedro*, Torquemada's willingness to tolerate Cruz's usurpation of his will vanishes; his hatred of her comes into the open, revealing bitter recalcitrance rather than comical opposition. Torquemada tells Pedro Gamborena, the former missionary who is now the spiritual advisor of the family, that he was more tranquil and more in his element in the old days; now his will does not prevail even in his own house (v, 1116–1117). Gamborena partially recognizes the legitimacy of Torquemada's complaints when he makes this accusation face-to-face with Cruz: "Tu despotismo, que despotismo es, aunque de los más ilustrados; tu afán de gobernar autocráticamente, contrariándole en sus hábitos y hasta en sus malas mañas, imponiéndole grandezas que repugna y dispendios que le fríen el alma, han puesto al salvaje en un grado tal de

7

ferocidad que nos ha de costar trabajillo desbravarle" (v, 1119).

Fidela's death intensifies Torquemada's detestation of Cruz; no longer is there a social bond to unite them (v, 1144, 1147, 1151, 1152–1153). When friction between the two reaches the point of combustion, Gamborena seeks to effect a reconciliation. This occurs at dinner one day and, although it amounts to nothing more than a temporary dampening of the fuel of Torquemada's hatred, his digestion, very poor of late, is much better than usual (v, 1159). They remain distant after the reconciliation and Cruz becomes largely indifferent to Torquemada's acts, such as the reduction by two-thirds of the household servants (v, 1160). By this time, however, the miser's stomach ailment has worsened to the point of becoming his principal preoccupation. He momentarily thinks he is being poisoned (v, 1164). Speaking to some of his cronies of the old days when he was a vulgar usurer, Torquemada in a confused play on words associates his indigestion with Cruz: ¡Ah! Puerta Cerrada se llama . . . , la cruz es ésta, no . . . , la otra . . . , [Cruz del Águila] y la Puerta Cerrada es la Cruz que yo tengo dentro de mi cuerpo y que no puedo echar fuera" (v, 1172). The enormous quantity of food consumed by Torquemada in the company of his old friends is the precipitating cause of his mortal illness.[14] His shrewd intuitive declaration as to the cause of his illness is the best diagnosis available; it is what psychologists now call a psychosomatic illness. This ailment which eventually leads to Torquemada's death is brought on by a bitter hatred of the woman who prevented him from expressing his inner self.

In his *A Dictionary of Psychology,* James Drever defines sublimation as "an unconscious process by which a sexual impulse, or its energy, is deflected, so as to express itself in some non-sexual, and socially acceptable, activity; often used loosely of any substitution of what appears to be a higher satisfaction for a lower."[15] Freud's contention that the displacement of energy that takes place in sublimation is never quite satisfactory for the individual, is expounded by Calvin S. Hall, a contemporary psychoanalyst: "Sublimation does not result in complete satisfaction; there is always some residual tension which cannot be discharged by sublimated object choices."[16] Galdós's anticipation of Freud in the presentation of sublimated love in his characters will be clearly demonstrated.

A case of sublimation is found in the portrayal of doña Paulita Porreño in *La Fontana de Oro* (1867–1868), Galdós's first full-length novel. The main facts about doña Paulita Porreño's conversion from excessive religious devotion to passionate human love have already been presented. Her conversion gives every indication of being a case of sublimation.

Galdós affirms the sincerity of doña Paulita's mysticism in his first description of her: "Examinando atentamente su figura, se observaba que la expresión mística que en toda ella resplandecía era más bien debida a un hábito de contracciones y movimientos que a natural y congénita forma. No se crea por eso que era hipócrita, no; era una verdadera santa, una santa por convicción y por fervor" (IV, 77). Don Benito goes on, however, to hint at complication in the saint's mysticism:

Pero había momentos, y de eso sólo el autor de este libro puede ser testigo; había momentos, decimos en que las pupilas de la santa irradiaban una luz y un calor extraordinarios. Y es que sin duda, el alma abrasada en amor divino se manifiesta siempre de un modo misterioso y con síntomas que el observador superficial no puede apreciar. (IV, 77)

Galdós first establishes the sincerity of doña Paulita, thus implying a subconscious factor in the subsequent development of her human love, then he subtly prepares the reader for such a development. The gradual mellowing of doña Paulita's personality as her love for Lázaro becomes more conscious has already been described. When Lázaro, who fits under the category of superficial observers mentioned by Galdós, praises doña Paulita for her sanctity, she protests: "No soy digna de veneración, sino de lástima—contestó con mucha amargura" (IV, 129). Later, in the same conversation she clarifies this statement, albeit not so much so that Lázaro is made aware that he is the object of doña Paulita's love:

9

> ¡Ay de aquellos que no se han conocido, que se han engañado a sí mismos y han dejado torcerse a la naturaleza y falsificarse el carácter sin reparar en ello! Esos cuando lo callado hable, cuando lo oculto salga, cuando lo disfrazado se descubra, serán víctimas de los más espantosos sufrimientos. Se sentirán nacer de nuevo en edad avanzada; notarán que han vivido muchos años sin sentido; notarán que el nuevo ser, originado por una tardía transformación, se desarrolla intolerante, orgulloso, pidiendo todo lo que le pertenece, lo que es suyo, lo que una vida ficticia y engañosa no le ha sabido dar; pidiendo sentimientos que el viejo ser, el ser inerte, indiferente y frío, no ha conocido. (IV, 129)

A more explicit description of doña Paulita's sublimation of sexual love would require that she be a psychologist. Since Galdós has already affirmed the sincerity of her mysticism, it may be inferred that *lo callado, lo oculto,* and *lo disfrazado,* of which doña Paulita speaks, refer to subconscious repressed impulses rather than consciously suppressed ones. The strength and nature of these impulses are, of course, revealed when she proposes that Lázaro flee with her (IV, 182).

In *Halma* (1895), the hardships which doña Catalina de Artal, condesa de Halma, undergoes after the death of her husband, influence her decision to retire to a convent. She is able to return to Spain from a Greek island where her husband died, only after much delay and abuse incurred at the hands of her brother-in-law (V, 1773–1775). Upon her arrival in Spain she is subject to further ill treatment by her brother, the marqués de Feramor and other relatives, who had objected to her marriage in the first place (V, 1771–1772, 1775). The author says that after the death of her husband, Halma accepted all of her privations "por amor de Cristo anhelando purificarse con el sufrimiento" (V, 1773).

The condesa's decision to leave the everyday world of affairs develops into a project with a more practical bent: possessed of a compassionate nature since early childhood, she decides to found a charitable institution under the auspices of the Church. She does so, bringing with her a parasitical childhood friend, José Antonio de Urrea, who she believes can be reformed, given loving care and the financial means of paying his debts. The enigmatic priest, Nazarín, who because of his efforts to imitate Christ in the modern world has caused considerable consternation and speculation as to his sanity, is also placed under the probationary care of Halma by ecclesiastical authorities. From the beginning José Antonio's reaction to Halma's compassionate treatment of him is one of gratitude and awe because of her great piety and generosity (v, 1831–1832). His thoughts of her are expressed in this way, indicating a certain idolizing of his benefactress: "Más que una mujer, Halma era una diosa, un ángel femenino" (v, 1839).

When members of the religious community advise Halma to send José Antonio back to Madrid because rumors of an amorous liaison between the condesa and her spiritual ward will damage the reputation of the community, Halma goes to Nazarín for advice on the matter. Nazarín tells Halma that she was attracted to mysticism by her imagination as a result of her disillusionment after the death of her husband, and because of the mistreatment by her relatives. He advises her to marry José Antonio, suggesting that she may have loved him since the first time he asked her for money (v, 1869–1870). Halma replies that she had interpreted José Antonio's affection as gratitude, but had suspected that there might be more to it (v, 1870).

The Necessity of Love

A basic psychological principle underlying Galdós's presentation of nearly all his characters, but which is particularly emphasized in some dozen or so characters, is the necessity of love of oneself and of others for the integration of personality. In all of the instances discussed here there is a deficit in either self-love or love of others. Nevertheless, Galdós's focus on the personality disintegration which results from such a deficit implies a positive ethic of love.

In *La familia de León Roch* (1878) the envy which the parasitical profligate don Agustín, marqués de Tellería, feels toward his morally circumspect son-in-law, León Roch, reveals a subtle form of self-hatred. When the father-in-law comes to León, a month after the latter's separation from his wife to borrow money and lecture him on the moral crime he has committed in abandoning María Egipciaca, his daughter, León turns the tables on the marqués by demonstrating his hypocrisy. After León's withering attack on the marqués's immorality, the latter feels that he could fit into a matchbox; it is evident that León lives on a much higher moral level than don Agustín (IV, 852–857).

Don Agustín's feeling of moral insignificance is arrested, however, by the sight of Monina, Pepa Fúcar's daughter. Since León lives on the estate of Pepa's father, and is known to have friendly relations with Pepa, the marqués hits upon the idea that León is the father of Monina. The description that Galdós gives of the moral expansion felt by the marqués upon conceiving this idea is a plastic one: "Algo muy grande sentía dentro de sí que, dilatándose, le hacía creer de tal modo que ya no cabía en la escalera, ni en el portal . . . , casi no cabía en la calle, ni en el campo, ni en el universo" (IV, 858). Galdós continues the commentary on don Agustín's feelings, disclosing the envy and ultimate self-hatred at the root of this attempted moral levelling: "¡Qué bueno es tener una idea, sobre todo cuando esa idea nos consuela de nuestra infamia con la infamia de los demás, haciéndonos exclamar con orgullo: ¡Todos somos lo mismo, lo mismo!" (IV, 858).

Don Agustín's desire to think and speak evil of León presupposes a conscience which is still active at least subconsciously, if not consciously, since his son-in-law is judged not to be living up to a moral standard which has a certain value in the marqués's mind. The latter himself does not live up to that implicit standard and is consoled by convincing himself that his son-in-law does not live up to it either. The dynamic factor in his urge to speak evil of León is his own conscious or subconscious realization that he has failed to meet the moral standard which he implicitly values. From this, it may be inferred that his envy, and desire to spread gossip ultimately arise from a veiled hatred of himself for failing to reach the subconsciously valued moral standard. One must love himself before he can love others. This is what Jesus meant when he said "love thy neighbor as thyself." Galdós, in his presentation of the marqués, reveals how the two loves are inextricably interrelated.

The death of the priest don Manuel Flórez in *Halma* is

the final result of an illness nurtured by his hatred of himself. His self-hatred stems from not having been more ardent in the practice of Christian charity, a shortcoming of which he feels he has become aware too late in life. The catalytic agents for his feeling of failure as a priest are Halma and Nazarín; Flórez feels himself pale into insignificance when he compares his perfunctory practice of charity with the fervent love for their fellow men demonstrated by these dedicated souls.

Flórez is a sympathetic priest who has achieved a facile success because of his ability to persuade people to his side by appealing to their interests and by using certain manipulative techniques without alienating them (v, 1782-1783). Since he is Halma's spiritual director, and because of his interest in her project of founding a charitable institution, Flórez appeals to the desire of her utilitarian brother to come off well in the eyes of others, to overlook a debt Halma owes him (v, 1786-1788), and persuades him to give her an old castle for her charitable undertaking (v, 1794-1795).

Flórez first has a feeling of inadequacy when he visits Nazarín and feels himself in the presence of a superior goodness. The priest tries to rationalize his wounded pride by telling himself that each has a separate function: he with the rich, Nazarín with the poor (v, 1815). Moreover, Halma's compassionate treatment of José Antonio Urrea, an incorrigible parasite in the eyes of everyone else, and her plans to establish a charitable institution give rise to further invidious comparisons (v, 1821-1822). When his niece and a servant call him a saint, Flórez responds: "¿Es tribulación andar de casa en casa festejado y en palmitas, aquí de servilleta prendida, allá charlando de mil variedades eclesiásticas y mundanas, metiéndome y sacándome con achaque de limosnitas, socorros y colectas, que son a la verdadera caridad lo que las comedias a la vida real?" (v, 1821-1822). The dying Flórez is aware of how he has departed from the path of Christ himself: "El era todo amor al género humano; yo, todo amor de mí mismo" (v, 1830). He goes on to call himself a "santo de salón." When Flórez dies shortly after these expressions of disillusionment, no physical diagnosis whatsoever has been made of the cause of his illness; it is obviously a psychological ailment; his death results from a belated awareness that he has been false to a better self.

The characters of Galdós who fail to love their fellow men invariably bring upon themselves a sort of psychological retribution which is disruptive to the harmonious functioning of their personality. A subconscious reaction to a failure to love is disclosed in *Casandra* (1905). Shortly after receiving the news that her wealthy aunt, doña Juana Samaniego, plans to leave her wealth to the church instead of to her needy relatives, her niece, Clementina de la Cerda, falls into a delirious state in which she addresses a friend, thinking the friend is her husband, Alfonso: "Desconfío de tu carácter, amamantado con la leche de la clemencia" (VI, 161). Clementina's subconscious desire for the death of doña Juana is repressed the following day and Clementina displays Christian resignation.

Once her subconscious desire is fulfilled when Casandra kills doña Juana, Clementina becomes particularly sensitive to comparisons between herself and Lady Macbeth made half in jest by the friend who overheard her delirious talk (VI, 184, 189, 199). Clementina reacts with greater horror than anyone else to the crime that benefitted her and doña Juana's other relatives. Clementina cannot admit, as do the other relatives, that she feels even as much as an equivocal happiness (VI, 185–186). Her subconscious feeling of guilt for having wished the death of doña Juana is further illustrated by the facility with which she succumbs to pressure from doña Juana's administrator, Cebrián, to contribute to the religious causes for which his former employer had intended to provide. Clementina explains her state of mind to her husband: "Me he visto asediada . . . , amenazada . . . Antes que a mi razón han hablado a mi conciencia . . . No puedo ocultarte que he sentido un pavor muy hondo . . . Yo creo en el Cielo y en el infierno . . . Quien cree, teme . . . , y más temeroso es quien no está libre de pecado" (VI, 201).

In the presentation of Clementina's guilt feelings, Galdós anticipates what psychoanalysts later called reaction formation. This is a psychological defense mechanism whereby an individual rejects subconscious impulses that are unaccept-

14

able to his conscience by consciously taking a strong stand contrary to his subconscious urges.

The individual who has insufficient self-love always harms himself, and often, but not always, does harm to others. How much harm such an individual does to others depends on the particular relationship he has with them. The characters in Galdós's novels who demonstrate insufficient love are usually considered better and more generous than others by their friends, who usually fail to see the deeper underlying defect of character from which this generosity proceeds.

Alejandro Miquis, one of the protagonists of *El doctor Centeno* (1883), is the prime example in Galdós's novels of inadequate self-love. This inadequacy occasions the neglect of his servant and friend, Felipe, and eventually leads to his own death.

Miquis, supposedly studying law in Madrid, lives a bohemian life and aspires to be a dramatist. He receives modest financial support from his Manchegan parents, and from Felipe's begging, and more substantial, albeit sporadic, aid from doña Isabel Godoy de Hinojosa, a great-aunt in Madrid. Her assistance is based on a desire to see someone exalt the family name. What Miquis does with the money he receives from these sources reveals his lack of charity toward himself and toward his servant.

Galdós makes it clear that Miquis's motives in taking on the teen-aged Felipe as a servant are mixed: "Con esto cumple Alejandro dos fines: el egoísmo de amparar al chico y ponerle al estudio" (IV, 1373). Miquis is too undisciplined to attend to the needs of the boy, and Felipe soon becomes the servant of all of Miquis's friends (IV, 1373). Furthermore, Alejandro puts him in a school too advanced for him, with the result that the boy becomes disillusioned with school (IV, 1373–1374). When Miquis becomes sick later, he is given sporadic aid by his equally undisciplined friends and by Felipe's begging. On one occasion when Miquis gives him three *duros* to repay a friend, Felipe, tired of wearing worn-out boots, spends the money on a new pair. When he returns home Miquis sees the new boots, only then realizing his neglect of his servant (IV, 1437).

While one final result of Miquis's lack of self-love is to reduce his servant and friend to a beggar, it brings on illness and ultimately death in his own case. When he first receives a substantial amount of money from his aunt, he is liberal to the point of extravagance (IV, 1363, 1364–1365). Galdós affirms his excessive generosity and reveals how his parasitical friends take advantage of these traits:

> Y derretía de lo lindo el dinero más en el prójimo que en sí mismo. Era un secuaz ardiente del Evangelio. Desde que un amigo se veía en apuro, lo que pasaba un día sí y otro no, ya le faltaba tiempo a Miquis para volar a socorrerle. Muchos— ¡tales traiciones tiene la amistad!—fingían penurias para sacarle dinero y gastarlo en francachelas (IV, 1380).

No sooner does Miquis receive money than it disappears. He soon falls prey to tuberculosis as a result of poor nutrition and unhealthy living quarters, to which he is forced to move because of his lack of money. Once after he has given some eggs to a friend which he himself badly needed, Galdós makes a remark which could be applied to his whole pattern of existence: "La naturaleza le pidió cuentas de su falta de caridad consigo mismo" (IV, 1407).

When Miquis dies at the end of the novel, it is evident that, in spite of his generosity toward others, his lack of "caridad consigo mismo" is the cause of his own destruction and also results in the neglect of Felipe. From this, it may be inferred that Galdós's view of charity that is not based on self-love ultimately results in more harm than good.

In *El abuelo* (1897) Lucrecia, condesa de Laín, the mother of the young ladies, Nell and Dolly, out of charity makes the weak-willed don Pío Coronado the private tutor of her daughters. The girls' mischievous, though unmalicious manipulation of the good-natured don Pío reveals the passiveness of his goodness. In one of his moments of depression don Pío explains to the conde de Albrit, the protagonist of the novel, his weakness of character:

> Nací para dejar que todo el mundo haga de mí lo que quiera. Soy un niño, señor conde, y no un niño de la raza humana, sino de la raza ovejuna; soy un cordero, aunque me esté mal el decirlo. Nací sin carácter, y sin carácter he llegado a viejo.

Permítame que me alabe. Soy el hombre más bueno del mundo; tan bueno, tan bueno que casi he llegado a despreciarme a mí mismo. (VI, 83–84)

He goes on to tell the conde how he is martyrized by his six daughters, who have not the least respect for him and dominated by his wife, whose very presence makes him tremble (VI, 84–85). The conde replies: "Buen Pío, tu filosofía resulta dañina: tu bondad siembra de males toda la tierra" (VI, 85). The evils to which the conde refers are the bad marriages made by don Pío's daughters against his wishes. Don Pío admits to the conde that his scorn of himself is so intense that, but for want of courage, he would hurl himself over the cliffs into the sea; nevertheless, he fearfully declines the conde's offer to hasten his entrance into paradise by pushing him over.

A brief allusion to the cause of the financial ruin of the conde de Albrit indicates that he himself may have a special reason for being able to sympathize so much with don Pío's predicament. As the conde is about to explain to the doctor that the cause of his ruin was not from doing harm to anyone, rather the contrary, the doctor interrupts him with these words: "Ya lo sé: del altruísmo desordenado, de no saber contenerse en la generosidad a todo bicho viviente" (VI, 93).

Self-Sacrifice

It may be argued with good reason that all of Galdós's characters are unique in their ability to love. It is also true that there are individual differences in a character's capacity for self-sacrifice.

In *Fortunata y Jacinta* (1886–1887), the priest, Nicolás Rubín considers himself particularly capable of advising young people on matters of love. In actuality he is inept in this role because of his indifference to physical love. Nicolás seizes with alacrity the suggestion that he talk with Fortunata in order to judge her potential for reform before she marries his brother, Maxi. Galdós makes this comment on the priest's particular ineptitude for such a task:

Aquel clérigo, arreglador de conciencias, que se creía médico de corazones dañados de amor, era quizá la persona más inepta para el oficio a que se dedicaba a causa de su propia virtud, estéril y glacial, condición negativa que, si le apartaba del peligro, cerraba sus ojos a la realidad del peligro del alma humana. Practicaba su apostolado por fórmulas rutinarias o rancios aforismos de libros escritos por santos como él y había hecho inmenso daño a la Humanidad arrastrando a doncellas incautas a la soledad de un convento, tramando casamientos entre personas que no se querían y desgobernando, en fin, la máquina admirable de las pasiones. (v, 216)

Nicolás's incapacity for physical love leads him to consider it an unreal type of love, and he tries to convince Fortunata of this: "El verdadero amor es el espiritual, y la única manera de amar es enamorarse de la persona por las prendas del alma" (v, 216). He adds: "No crea en otro amor que en el espiritual, o sea en las simpatías de alma con alma" (v, 216).[17]

Another character in *Fortunata y Jacinta,* the philanthropic doña Guillermina Pacheco, unlike Nicolás, is aware that Fortunata's marriage to Maximiliano will involve a sacrifice since the young woman feels no physical attraction toward him; yet because she exalts sacrifice as an ideal and challenge, she advises Fortunata to marry him: "Al cumplir ciertos deberes, cuando el amor no facilita el cumplimiento, es la mayor hermosura del alma. . . . ¿Cuál es la mayor de las virtudes? La abnegación, la renuncia de la felicidad. ¿Qué es lo que mas purifica a la criatura? El sacrificio" (v, 397–398).

While there can be little doubt that Leré's religious vocation is authentic in *Angel Guerra* (1890–1891), there is also evidence that her religious vocation may be easier for her than it would be for most people. The cruel treatment which Leré, her physically abnormal brother, and her mother received at the hands of her drunken father when she was a child has given her a negative attitude toward marriage (v, 1260). She sometimes speaks with repugnance of marriage, and at other times reveals a complete indifference to physiological needs (v, 1261, 1282, 1344). Leré herself is aware of this aversion to sexual involvement with men and feels that there is no merit in her ability to keep herself pure since there is no temptation (v, 1294).

What Leré fails to realize is the enormous force of Angel Guerra's sexual drive; he deceives her as well as himself. When Angel is dying Leré asks for his forgiveness if she has caused him harm by encouraging him to assume a religious vocation too austere for his personality make-up (v, 1531). She has been blinded by the great gulf existing between her needs and those of Angel.

Don Tomé, the chaplain of a convent in Toledo, is something of a male counterpart to Leré in *Angel Guerra*. Angel takes an interest in the seraphic, childlike don Tomé in the early stages of his own religious development since the chaplain seems to have overcome all strivings of the flesh, a goal pursued by Angel. As don Tomé lies dying, however, he discloses to Angel that he really has not had to struggle against the flesh: "Me creerá usted cuando le diga que en mí no existe ni ha existido jamás nada que ni remotamente trascienda a sensaciones de amor físico o sensual. El señor me hizo este beneficio desde que me puso en el mundo" (v, 1451). He later adds: "Yo no soy mujer, pero tampoco hombre: soy un serafín" (v, 1451).

This, then, is love from the psychological perspective in Galdós's novels. It has been demonstrated that from Galdós's viewpoint love is an extremely dynamic force in the individual; the presence or absence of love, or the presence of hate invariably influences the conduct of the individual. Furthermore, such a view presupposes a conception of personality in conformance with which the individual has a relatively stable inner self which may not be violated without psychological repercussions. The need to love and to be loved is an essential and permanent part of this inner self; when this need is met, the individual thrives as a full human being, when not, he suffers not only a disintegration of his personality, but also a diminution of his humanity.

Notes

[1]"Galdós and Abnormal Psychology," *Hispania,* 23 (1940): 27–36.

[2]"A Study of the Abnormal Characters in the Novels of Benito Pérez Galdós" (Diss., Cornell University, 1949).

[3]"Estudio preliminar y bibliografía" to *Miau* by Benito Pérez Galdós (1957), pp. 211–225.

[4]*Dreams in the Novels of Galdós* (1960). Schraibman's study of dreams includes normal as well as abnormal characters.

[5]*Obras completas,* ed. Federico Carlos Sainz de Robles (1941–1944). All references to the text of Galdós's novels are to the last three volumes: IV (3rd ed., 1954); V (3rd ed., 1961); VI (2nd ed., 1961). The volume and page numbers of references to the *Obras Completas* are included in the text of the study unless they are so lengthy as to unduly interrupt the text.

[6]In Sherman Eoff, *The Modern Novel* (1961), p. 143, brief mention has been made of the importance which Galdós attributes to a "natural 'given', the core of individuality which escapes determinism from without." Eoff bases this comment on two or three passages in Galdós's novels and other writings in which the importance of temperament or innate qualities is stressed. He does not, however, cite any evidence that this belief in an inner core of personality is implicit in Galdós's presentation of his characters, nor does he discuss the implications of such a conception of personality. See also Eoff, *The Novels of Pérez Galdós: The Concept of Life as Dynamic Process* (1954), pp. 24–25.

[7]There is no intention in the foregoing discussion to imply that Galdós consciously held such a view of personality. Whether he did or not is immaterial to the discussion here, since such a view is hypothetically implicit in his novels. It may at least be considered to be one of Galdós's "creencias" in the sense that José Ortega y Gasset uses the word in his *Ideas y creencias,* 8th ed. (1959), pp. 3–10.

[8]For similar statements by doña Paulita, see IV, 128, 180.

[9]In a letter to his father, Pepe gives the same explanation for his newly acquired tendency toward hatred and violence (IV, 491–492).

[10]IV, 478. As an interesting sidelight, David T. Sisto in "Pérez Galdós' *Doña Perfecta* and Louis Bromfield's *A Good Woman,*" *Symposium,* 14 (1957): 276, states: "We can be sure that Doña Perfecta's ultimate hatred arises from a subconscious desire to avenge the suffering caused by the former dissipation of her worthless husband of years ago." This assertion is certainly in harmony with Galdós's psychology of hatred, and all of the ingredients for the development of this motivational factor are present, but there is no indication that Galdós was interested in developing it.

[11]V, 525–526. He is later calmed down by his friend, Ballester, who persuades him to give up the gun.

[12]V, 1053. Cruz is also motivated by her desire to rise in rank and status above certain relatives, who ignored her family after its financial ruin and have spread malicious rumors about the del Aguila's alliance with Torquemada (V, 1053, 1054–1055, 1072).

[13]See, for example, V, 1019, 1021, 1030, 1044, 1045, 1046–1047, 1052–1053, 1080–1081, 1104, 1105.

[14]The doctor, Augusto Miquis, speculates on "algo de enteroptose, algo de cáncer del piloro" as the cause of Torquemada's illness, but Galdós declares that "nada podía afirmarse aún, como no fuera la gravedad y

casi la inutilidad final de los esfuerzos de la ciencia" (v, 1174). Nothing more is said about the physical cause of Torquemada's illness after this.

[15](1955), p. 381.

[16]*A Primer of Freudian Psychology* (1955), p. 83.

[17]Here, Galdós is implicitly indicting those priests who, because of deficiencies in their own personality make-up, give advice overlooking the natural needs of healthy human beings. They see a dichotomy between man's natural needs and his spiritual needs and consider the former as something base to be suppressed or gotten rid of altogether.

II   Charity and Society

ALTHOUGH GALDÓS'S NOVELS are quite frequently psychological studies, they are never only that; he always strives to
portray his characters interacting convincingly with other
characters in a well-defined social environment. One critic
who has studied his novels from the social perspective makes
this comment: "No one can fail to be impressed by Galdós's
marked attention to human associations. He is unmistakably
a social novelist, and the primary significance of his mission
as an artist and intellectual leader lies in his understanding
portrayal of man as a being who moves always within society, deeply affected, for better or for worse."[1]

Galdós's basic attitude toward organized charity appears
not to have changed during his long career. If clear-cut
differences exist between the *Novelas de la primera época*
and the *Novelas españolas contemporáneas,* they are seen in
the manner in which the theme of charity is presented. In
the contemporary novels, organized charity is found contrasted
to individual service so that a variety of viewpoints is found
more often in the individual novels of this group than in
the earlier novels (*Marianela* is an exception). Furthermore,
in the contemporary view charity based on individual initiative is given a positive value.

Social Injustice and Charity

Galdós would agree with the sociologist Frederick Howard
Wines, who made this observation on the nature of the
relationship between justice and charity: "Charity is a fine
thing no doubt; but justice is a finer. Justice is fundamental,
charity is supplemental. Charity steps in to relieve the situa-

tion where justice has partially failed."[2] Galdós's novels reveal that where social justice is absent to a great degree, charity becomes disproportionately stressed in spite of its patent inability to fill the gap. Galdós does not condemn charity, of course, but deplores the social organization and customs which make charity necessary. He condemns the attitude which allows the individual to be complacent about social injustice simply because he contributes to charity. He condemns the values of a society which considers spending enormous sums of money on inconsequential diversions more important than providing good schools for its children.

Evidence of social injustice is found throughout *El audaz,* (1871), and a couple of incidents reveal the attitude of the rich when confronted with particular instances of it. The revolutionary protagonist, Martín Muriel, appears at the mansion of the wealthy conde de Cerezuelo demanding justice, in this instance, a sum of money rightfully belonging to his father. He died miserably in a jail after the conde had dismissed him from his job because of false charges brought by a man who wanted to replace him. The justice of Muriel's claim is denied and he is obliquely offered charity instead. It is true, of course, that Muriel's manner of demanding justice is antagonistic, but his resentment of the wrongs which he and his family have suffered leads him to reject moderation, not to mention the meekness required by the conde in order to qualify for charity. The conde's condescending reply to Muriel's demand exhibits his inability or unwillingness to remedy the situation on any terms other than those of charity: "¡Qué manera tan singular de pedirme que le proteja! Viniendo de otra manera, yo le hubiera dado una limosna" (IV, 285). When the conde interprets Muriel's demand for justice, i.e., what is rightfully due him, as a request for protection, he reveals the bias of his class, which takes social inequities for granted and soothes the conscience with token charity.

Later, when Susana, the daughter of the conde, convinced that Muriel has talent, tries to persuade him to give up his revolutionary ideas in order to become a conventional success, he sees the basic humiliation that would be the price of such success: "Entonces no habrá personas que se aver-

23

güencen de ser benévolas conmigo. . . . Entonces no se me humillará ni habrá nadie que se crea exento de tener para conmigo y los míos aquellas consideraciones que la caridad exige" (IV, 322). Both the conde and his daughter refuse not only to think in terms of justice, but they also espouse a charity which is condescending by nature in that it requires the humiliation of the beneficiary.

In *Fortunata y Jacinta* Galdós uses the charitableness of Jacinta and doña Guillermina Pacheco as an indirect means of commenting on social injustice. After a visit to a factory during her honeymoon, Jacinta is moved to make these remarks:

> No puedes figurarte—decía a su marido, al salir de un taller— cuánta lástima me dan esas infelices muchachas que están ahí ganando un triste jornal, con el cual no sacan ni para vestirse. No tienen educación, son como máquinas y se vuelven tan tontas . . . , se vuelven tan tontas, digo, que en cuanto se les presenta un pillo cualquiera se dejan seducir. (v, 54)

Later, When Jacinta expresses her astonishment at the social inequality evident during a visit with doña Guillermina to a poor neighborhood, the latter replies: "La falta de educación es para el pobre una desventaja mayor que la pobreza" (v, 80).[3]

Doña Guillermina demonstrates by words and deeds that the proper treatment of the poor, given the social injustice that makes their condition difficult to remedy, includes an indulgent charitableness. After stripping the illiterate José Izquierdo of all of his pretensions when he tries to foist a counterfeit child upon Jacinta, Guillermina makes this comment to Jacinta in the presence of Izquierdo, mitigating his culpability: "Después—anadió la santa—, el pobre hombre ha tenido que valerse de mil arbitrios no muy limpios para poder vivir, porque es preciso vivir. . . . Hay que ser indulgentes con la miseria y otorgarle un poquitín de licencia para el mal" (v, 123). Guillermina shows how the poor should be treated when she offers Izquierdo a job as a doorman—refused by him out of a false sense of pride—gives him two *duros,* and advises him to continue to serve as a model for sculptors and painters since he has a finely shaped head.[4]

Through the enchantment in *El caballero encantado* (1909) of the thoughtless and dissolute young aristocrat, don Carlos de Tarsis, Galdós is able to comment indirectly on a variety of social evils in Spain. The enchantment of the protagonist gives the novelist the license to disregard the demands of verisimilitude, so meticulously fulfilled in his other novels, in order to present a panoramic view of Spain's principal social evils and to present as a solution to these ills, love and understanding. Don Carlos's name is changed under the influence of enchantment, and he is switched rapidly from one place to another as befits the novelist's intention to survey dramatically the principal problems of Spain.

Early in the novel, don Carlos is shown raising the rent of his impoverished tenant farmers in order to be able to lead the life of a libertine in Madrid (VI, 227). Don Carlos, whose new name is Gil, has as his first occupation under the spell of enchantment, the work of a farm laborer. He tells a venerable white-haired lady that he realizes that he has been made a farm laborer in order to learn that the wealth he squanders so lightly is hard to come by—it is produced by the sweat of the brow. The lady assents to this and reproaches him for having raised his tenants' rent (VI, 251-252). Thus, Gil is to acquire understanding, if not love, of those who work with their hands, by doing what they do and feeling what they feel.

Later in his travels, Gil encounters an ancient school teacher, don Alquiborontifosio, who lives by begging, though he gives most of what comes into his hands to the school children (VI, 297). In a subsequent chance encounter with the school teacher, Gil learns that two generations of Gaitines, the local *caciques,* have neglected him (VI, 316). Here, Galdós is attacking a society which foolishly leaves justice in the hands of *caciques* with the result that teachers are reduced to begging for a living.

Another character in this novel, don Venancio, a priest, sees charitable giving as less meritorious than social justice: "Cuando damos con qué subsistir a los que están en necesidad, no les damos lo que es nuestro; ¡les damos lo que es suyo!" (VI, 300). Such a view implies the priority of social justice to charity.[5]

Charity as a Producer of Vice

Although certain characters in Galdós's novels hold dogmatically the view that charity foments vice, the position of the novelist himself on this matter is not so simple. In some cases charity does produce vice and parasitism, in others it does not. Galdós presents a wide variety of parasites, ranging from the relatively harmless individual, to whole families who descend upon the unwary philanthropist, decimating his fortune.

In *La familia de León Roch* (1878) León marries into a family of parasites and neurotics when he marries María Egipciaca Tellería. Her father and mother, don Agustín and doña Milagros, and her brother Leopoldo are a constant drain on León's financial resources. Two of María's other brothers, Luis Gonzaga and Gustavo, are not parasites, but reveal neurotic tendencies. An examination of the charity which León bestows upon the Tellerías discloses nothing that is positive except his intention.

In spite of her failure to pay León the three thousand *duros* she owes him, Milagros, unabashed, goes to him for three thousand more (IV, 784). Shortly afterwards, Leopoldo comes to León for a second loan of four thousand *reales* (IV, 790). León pities him because his dissipation harms himself more than anyone else. Added to this are the importunate pleas for money of don Agustín, who successfully seeks to move León to pity by claiming that he is being sued (IV, 853). None of the Tellerías discreetly uses the money given to them: on the contrary, it is consumed in luxuries by Milagros and through dissipation by the two male parasites. León finally awakens to the necessity to be more discreet in his generosity when don Agustín comes to ask for money even after the former has already separated from María. Before offering don Agustín a lifetime pension, which is refused out of pride, León redefines his generosity toward the Tellerías: "Lo que yo he hecho no es generosidad, señor marqués: es un verdadero crimen. No he amparado a menesterosos, sino que he protegido el vicio" (IV, 854).[6]

Tormento (1884) and *La de Bringas* (1884) are considered together here since Francisco Bringas and his wife Rosalía play major roles in both of these novels. Don Francisco is a bureaucrat who relies upon the state to provide his necessities, while he and his wife look to his rich and generous cousin, Agustín Caballero, to provide them with certain luxuries. Don Francisco's parasitism does not go beyond accepting Agustín's offer to pay for his daughter's piano lessons and his children's schooling (IV, 1466, 1510). Rosalía, on the other hand, is less modest in her designs on Agustín's money; the thought actually passes through her mind that she would marry Agustín were her husband to die (IV, 1471). Rosalía even takes advantage of Agustín's indulgent generosity to enter his house and remove vases, writing paper, and shirts (IV, 1565–1566). And when Agustín, because of circumstances, decides to take Amparo Sánchez Emperador to live unmarried with him in France, Rosalía, envious and angry, has the lack of self-insight to fix the epithet of "sanguijuela" on the woman who really loves him (IV, 1569). In spite of their expressed indignation at Agustín's flight with Amparo, neither of the Bringas consider themselves sufficiently offended to reject Agustín's parting gift of the articles that had been bought for the ill-fated wedding (IV, 1569).

In *La de Bringas,* the narrator comments that the gifts of Agustín had created in Rosalía a taste for the luxury of dressing well. The blame is attributed half playfully to Agustín:

> Después de haber estrenado tantos y tan hermosos trajes, ¿cómo resignarse a volver a los trapitos antiguos y a no variar nunca de moda? Esto no podía ser. Aquel bendito Agustín había sido, generosamente y sin pensarlo, el corruptor de su prima; había sido la serpiente de buena fé que le metió en la cabeza las más peligrosas vanidades que pueden ahuecar el cerebro de una mujer. Los regalitos fueron la fruta cuya dulzura le quitó la inocencia, y por culpa de ellos un ángel con espada de raso me la echó de aquel Paraíso tan sujeta. (IV, 1587–1588)

In the case of Rosalía, it may be argued with good reason that Agustín's charity is misdirected; where the benefits are received by the children, the case is less clear since the reader is not apprised of the results of their schooling and the piano lessons.

This is true, at least, with the possible exception of the eldest son, Paquito, who at the age of sixteen already holds a job in the treasury department. Of Paquito's studies, it is known that they are not of such magnitude that they hinder him from making periodical visits to pick up his salary at his office, while they are sufficiently time-consuming to rule out his actually working for that salary (IV, 1574).

The idea of the state as a charitable mammal to be milked by all comers also constitutes a part of the characterization in *La de Bringas* of don Manuel Pez, a bureaucrat of some influence:

> Era este Pez el hombre más correcto que se podía ver, modelo excelente del empleado que llaman *alto* porque le toca ración grande en el repartimiento de limosnas que hace el Estado. . . . Para él, la Administración era una tapadera de formulas baldías, creada para encubrir el sistema práctico del favor personal, cuya clave está en el cohecho y las recomendaciones. (IV, 1593)

The tone in which this description is given makes further comment superfluous.[7]

Still another character in *La de Bringas* contributes to the theme of parasitism. What appears to be unselfish solicitude on the part of doña Cándida, widow of García Grande, is actually a stratagem for loosening the purse strings of the Bringas. When don Francisco suffers a temporary blindness, doña Cándida runs errands to the pharmacy on his behalf. Just when Rosalía is congratulating herself on having such a devoted friend, doña Cándida asks her for a loan of ten *duros,* which Rosalía reluctantly gives her because of the services she has rendered (IV, 1610). Hypocrisy is typical of doña Cándida's parasitism; more will be said about her later in this chapter when charity in *El amigo Manso* is discussed.

In *Lo prohibido* (1884–1885) several members of the Bueno de Guzmán family take advantage of the generosity of their rich cousin, José María Bueno de Guzmán, with the result that a sizable dent is made in his fortune.

Raimundo receives "charity" from the state as well as from his cousin. Like Paquito de Bringas in *La de Bringas,* Raimundo has a small bureaucratic job and appears only to pick up his monthly salary (IV, 1692). When he runs out of money because of the disorderly life he leads, he comes to José María, entertains him for a while with his agile conversation and clever drawings, then lets him know that he needs money (IV, 1688–1692, 1801). José María indicates that there are several motives for his generosity toward Raimundo: "La compasión, el parentesco, la admiración del ingenio de Raimundo, obraban en mí para determinar mi liberalidad" (IV, 1751). Raimundo claims that illness hinders him from working, but the truth is that the onset of his neurotic symptoms usually coincides with his running out of money (IV, 1692).

José María's conquest of the virtue of his married cousin, Eloísa, is facilitated by his catering to her taste for luxuries.[8] Perversely attracted to Eloísa by the charm of forbidden pleasures, José María loses interest in her when her husband dies. Her habit of high living formed, Eloísa bounces from one lover to another in an effort to continue living amidst her usual luxuries. When José María later loses most of what is left of his reduced fortune, his resentment of the part Eloísa had in diminishing it is such that he vehemently refuses any financial aid from her (IV, 1883).

When José María has tired of Eloísa and dedicates himself to the amorous conquest of her sister, Camila, he follows the same strategy of buying gifts for her. Camila, however, fails to succumb to the temptation of luxury. She accepts gifts reluctantly and only when her husband, Constantino, can share the gift or tells her to accept it (IV, 1767, 1779–1780, 1862, 1889). After José María's fall, when he is in a helpless paralyzed condition, Constantino and Camila are matchless in their solicitous care of him (IV, 1887–1888, 1882, 1889), in spite of Constantino's recently acquired knowledge that his friend has tried to seduce his wife. The dying José María is then moved by the unalloyed compassion which the couple have for him, and he makes them the principal beneficiaries of his will (IV, 1882, 1889).

The imprudent generosity of José María is contrasted with the discreet charity of Cristóbal Medina, the husband of Juana María, the older sister of Eloísa and Camila. Cristóbal loaned Eloísa money knowing it was lost and displeased his wife by refusing to take any of her luxurious furniture in compensation (IV, 1819). But he will help her only once. José María agrees with the wisdom of Cristóbal's cautious charity, but is incapable of imitating it:

> Cristóbal era generoso cuando veía una lástima y el lastimado no le pedía nada. Si otorgaba favores de todo corazón a algún prójimo, hacíalo por una vez; pero si el tal repetía, negábase resueltamente. He oído contar esta misma costumbre del barón Rothschild y de don José Salamanca, y me parece con perdón de los pedigüenos, que está basada en un sólido principio de moral financiera. (IV, 1819–1820)

Proof of the wisdom of this custom is dramatized in the novel in the respective reactions of Raimundo, Eloísa, and Camila to José María's generosity. The tendency of charity to promote vice, then, depends upon the personality of the beneficiary.

In *La Loca de la casa* (1892), Galdós brings into direct conflict a character who detests any form of compassion, because he sees only its negative effects, with a character who emanates compassion from every pore in her body. Pepet Cruz, who by dint of hard work and sheer ability, has amassed a fortune in America, returns to Spain with hopes of marrying one of the daughters of his now bankrupt former employer, don Juan de Moncada. The younger of the latter's two daughters is incapable of making the sacrifice of marrying the mannerless, materialistic Cruz in order to save her father. The older daughter Victoria is up to such a sacrifice, however, and abandons the convent to save her father and the people who depend upon him for their material support. Victoria thrives on self-sacrifice and charity and has always sought out the most repugnant tasks as a novitiate. Cruz marries Victoria and is gradually tamed, at least externally, to a less recalcitrant opposition to charitable acts.

30

When a relative of the Moncadas tells Cruz that she has heard that he has never given alms in his life, he replies: "No, señora, no las doy en secreto ni en público. No quiero proteger la mendicidad, que es lo mismo que fomentar la vagancia y los vicios" (v, 1625). Cruz then adds: "¡La compasión! . . . Lo sé por experiencia . . . ; es una flaqueza del ánimo que siempre nos trae algún perjuicio. ¡La compasión! Dondequiera que arrojen esa semilla verán nacer la ingratitud" (v, 1625). Cruz goes on to paint a picture of charity which would fit a Darwinian or Nietzschean view of economics:[9]

Digo que la compasión, según yo lo he visto, aquí principalmente desmoraliza a la Humanidad, y le quita el vigor para las grandes luchas con la Naturaleza. De ahí viene, no lo duden, este sentimentalismo, que todo lo agosta; el incumplimiento de las leyes, el perdón de los criminales, la elevación de los tontos, el poder inmenso de la influencia personal, la vagancia, el esperarlo todo de la amistad y las recomendaciones, la falta de puntualidad en el comercio, la insolvencia . . . Por eso no hay ley ni crédito; por eso no hay trabajo, ni vida, ni nada . . . Claro, ustedes habituados ya a esta relajación, hechos a lloriquear por el prójimo, no ven las verdaderas causas del acabamiento de la raza, y todo lo resuelven con limosnas, aumentando cada día el numero de mendigos, de vagos y de trapisondistas. (v, 1625)[10]

Victoria begins her softening of Cruz before she marries him. She makes her agreement to marry him contingent upon the fulfillment of certain conditions, not the least of which are specified acts of charity such as restoring the credit and business of her father and bringing up and educating the six children of a deceased relative, hitherto supported by Moncada. One part of the pact—that in case of grave disagreement the wife will return to her paternal home—is put into effect by Victoria a few months after the marriage. Victoria considers Cruz's refusal to respect her right to give a certain quantity of money to the indigent mother of Daniel Malavella a breach of the agreement made before the marriage and consequently returns to her father's home. By this time she and Cruz are mutually in love and can hardly bear living apart, but Victoria remains firm and Cruz must compromise. The conditions set by Victoria for terminating the separation involve, among other things, earmarking large sums of Cruz's money for charitable purposes. Cruz is persuaded rather mercilessly to concede one-fifth of the shares of one of his banks to Victoria's father. He is also forced to build two schools, endow a hospital, finish building an orphanage, and give a home to the marquesa de Malavella, who has no means of supporting herself (v, 1672–1676). In short, he is persuaded to perform acts of charity which conflict with his materialistic philosophy of life.

Galdós is far from condemning the arguments used by Cruz to condemn the effects in Spain of too much compassion and charity; on the contrary, he uses these arguments to condemn only the negative aspects of charity. Unlike Cruz, he does not condemn charity per se because it has bad consequences when practiced without discretion. The charity which Cruz is gradually led to practice cannot be said to produce vice, since it is directed toward orphaned children, the sick, and the ostensibly circumspect Moncada family.

Institutional Charity

Aside from governmental agencies two kinds of institutional charity appear in Galdós's novels: that organized by more or less formal social groups such as associations or the church, and charity which has its origin primarily in the initiative of individuals.

Although the concern here is with charity as presented in Galdós's novels, the Spanish novelist has made comments more substantial than hints about his attitude toward organized charity. In "Crónica de Madrid" after a cholera epidemic in 1865, he praises those charitable organizations which provided quick aid to the victims of the epidemic:

También merecen agradecimiento público todas las sociedades de socorros, que, con una abnegación digna de ser imitada, han organizado un sistema de beneficencia domiciliaria que, sin ser tan complicada como la oficial y sin tener la múltiple ramificación, adornada con todo el expediente y la tramitación de las oficinas, surte efectos más directos, porque es más espontánea e hija tan sólo de un sentimiento de caridad, que no es el que más abunda en las regiones burocráticas. (VI, 1536)

Earlier in the same year when he was writing of the circulation of counterfeit money in "Crónica de Madrid," don Benito had used the occasion to criticize other counterfeit aspects of society: "Si corre por esos mundos [Madrid] el estaño disfrazado de plata, también anda por ahí la filantropía haciéndose pasar por caridad" (VI, 1521).

A study of Galdós's novels reveals that the novelist is critical of organized charity which requires the intervention of some sort of bureaucracy for the distribution of its benefits to the needy. Don Benito is also critical of charity which, because it is organized principally for motives other than compassion for the unfortunate, permits the organizers to feel self-righteous in spite of having felt no real concern for those toward whom the charity is directed, and in spite of having overlooked their real needs. The man who would help his neighbor must know what his neighbor needs. Galdós agrees with the biblical epigram that "man does not live by bread alone." There are those who would sate the stomach and starve the soul; don Benito requires not only that compassion be guided by knowledge, but also that knowledge be used for compassionate ends.

In *Marianela* (1878) Galdós's attitude toward organized charity revealed in the relationships of Marianela (Nela) with several other characters in the novel is one of the more important facets of his viewpoint with respect to charity. Nela is an orphan about seventeen years old who, too weak for heavy work, passes her time in the mining town of Socartes serving as a guide and companion to the blind Pablo Penáguilas. Through the cheerful, lyrical spontaneity of her personality, the homely Nela convinces Pablo that she is beautiful and he promises her that they will always remain together. This idyl is interrupted, however, by the arrival in Socartes of Teodoro Golfín, an able surgeon and brother of the chief engineer of the mining company in the town. Golfín performs an operation curing Pablo of his blindness, and Pablo consents to his father's wish that he marry his beautiful cousin Florentina Penáguilas, forgetting

33

the promise he made to Nela. Nela dies of grief when Pablo, seeing her for the first time, is unable to suppress a spontaneous cry of shock and disappointment at her ugliness.

Nela is given a place to sleep in various corners of the Centenos' house, where she is treated with less deference than the family cat, which at least hears kind words from time to time (IV, 694–695, 698). The mistress of the house, Señana, provides comfortable beds for their two children who work in the mines, because they bring in money for the family coffer (IV, 697). Nela's minimum physical needs are met, but her need for affection and tenderness is completely neglected. Galdós says this of Señana's attitude toward the orphan: "Nunca se le dió a entender que tenía derecho, por el mismo rigor de la Naturaleza al criarla, a ciertas atenciones de que pueden estar exentos los robustos, los sanos, los que tienen padres y casa propia, pero que corresponden por jurisprudencia cristiana al inválido, al pobre, al huérfano y al desheredado" (IV, 698). In spite of treating Marianela as if she were an object, Señana congratulates herself on her charity: "Repetidas veces dijo para sí, al llenar la escudilla de la Nela: 'Qué bien me gano mi puestecillo en el cielo'" (IV, 698).

As a result of this treatment Nela accepts Señana's verdict as to her basic worth (IV, 698, 715). When Nela tells Golfín later that she is worthless, he replies with these words, implying the responsibility of society in general in causing her to have such a conception of herself: "Esa idea de que no sirves para nada es causa de grandes desgracias para ti, ¡infeliz criatura! ¡Maldito sea el que te la inculcó, o los que te la inculcaron, porque son muchos!" (IV, 740).

One of the principal targets of Golfín's criticism is the wife of his brother, Sofía, who he felt should have done something to take Nela out of the misery in which she lives. Sofía's chief occupation consists in organizing dances and dramas for the benefit of the poor in general, while she remains indifferent to the misery at her feet. When Golfín points out to Sofía that it might have been better had she bought some shoes for the barefooted Nela instead of having bought a coat for her dog, she laughingly replies that the shoes would not have lasted two days and boasts that no one surpasses her in practicing a prudent charity (IV, 712). Golfín is unimpressed by Sofía's charity; he replies:

> Todo eso sólo me prueba las singulares costumbres de una sociedad que no sabe ser caritativa sino bailando, toreando y jugando a la lotería. No hablemos de eso; ya conozco estas heroicidades y las admiro; también esto tiene su mérito, y no poco. Pero tú y tus amigas rara vez acercáis a un pobre para saber de su boca la causa de su miseria . . . , ni para observar qué clase de miseria le aqueja, pues hay algunas tan extraordinarias, que no se alivian con la fácil limosna del ochavo ni tampoco con el mendrugo de pan. (IV, 714)

Golfín asserts that the problem of orphans will never be completely resolved, but would at least be alleviated if a law were passed providing every orphan with the right to be adopted into a home without children (IV, 715). Since Sofía and Carlos are childless. Sofía is correct in assuming that Golfín is implying criticism of them for not having adopted Nela.

When Nela gets a thorn in her foot retrieving Sofía's dog, the respective attitudes of the doctor and his sister-in-law toward the poor and helpless are vividly dramatized. Sofía protests that she cannot bear the sight of blood and goes ahead on the path, while Golfín extracts the thorn from the girl's foot. He then carries her on his shoulder the remaining distance to be travelled.[11] Sofía, in spite of her organized charity, reveals not only a callous indifference to individual suffering, but also an active aversion to witnessing the relief given by someone else, whereas Golfín is filled with compassion for the helpless. Golfín represents science with compassion,[12] while Sofía represents organized charity devoid of love for those it purports to help. It should be remembered too, that Señana's cruelty toward Nela, mistakenly interpreted as charity, is possible because the former lacks the perspective that accrues from knowledge. Galdós's attitude toward organized charity in this novel is similar to that expressed around the turn of the century by a sociologist: "But the physician who is not thoroughly grounded in anatomy is a sciolist and his practice can only be empirical. So the philanthropist who has taken no pains to know what may be and is known of social structure and function is no better than a social quack—certainly an ignoramus, and possibly impostor as well."[13]

Florentina, Pablo's fiancée, proposes to treat Nela as her equal and sister, thus providing her with the warmth and affection so lacking in her relations with Señana and Sofía. She makes this comment about her intention to help Nela, which reveals her greater awareness of the real needs of the poor:

> Para esto no basta vestir a una persona, ni sentarla delante de una mesa donde haya sopa y carne. Es preciso ofrecerle también aquella limosna que vale más que todos los mendrugos y que todos los trapos imaginables, y es la consideración, la dignidad, el nombre. Yo daré a mi pobre estas cosas, infundiéndole el respeto y la estimación de sí mismo. (IV, 732)

Despite Florentina's good intentions, she fails, for Nela is unable to bear the humiliation of having Pablo know that she is ugly. This humiliation, added to the many others that she has sustained throughout the years, crushes Nela's tenuous will to live. Florentina's only compensation is to help other poor people (IV, 751) and to give Nela a decent burial (IV, 755).

The theme of self-fulfillment through service to others is given considerable prominence in *El amigo Manso* (1882). The novel dramatizes a spectrum of various types of service ranging from giving advice to organized charity, and the spectrum extends to the evident opposites of service to mankind: selfishness and parasitism. Service which involves face-to-face contact between the benefactor and the beneficiary is held up for admiration; organized charity, egotism, and parasitism are satirized.

The message of self-fulfillment through service is conveyed through the words and deeds of the protagonist and narrator of the novel, Máximo Manso, a philosophy professor. Manso falls in love with Irene, a young lady whom he had known since she was sent as a child to his house to beg in behalf of the parasitical doña Cándida, the widow of García Grande. Creating Irene in the image of his own abstractions, Manso mistakenly sees her as superior to the general run of Spanish women and attributes desirable qualities to her which she is far from possessing. When he realizes his mistake, he feels even more attracted to her, but is able to control his feelings because he knows that Irene and his former pupil, Manolo Peña, are in love with each other. Furthermore, he has developed the habit of helping in a disinterested fashion those about him, and it is with such impartial benevolence that he sets about, after determining that it is the best solution, to facilitate the marriage of Irene and Manolo.

The first service rendered by Manso is his undertaking of the private education of Manolo at the request of the prospective student's mother, doña Javiera, a neighbor and admirer of Manso. Manolo's success in the academic world has been considerably short of brilliant until this time, since his teachers have been unimaginative bores, who have had neither enthusiasm for what they taught nor interest in their pupils (IV, 1171-1172). Under Manso's tutelage, Manolo awakens to a new interest in learning and his teacher gives this explanation for the change: "Desde el primer día conocí que inspiraba a mí discípulo no sólo respeto, sino simpatía; feliz circunstancia, pues no es verdadero maestro el que no se hace querer de sus alumnos, ni hay enseñanza posible sin la bendita amistad, que es el mejor conductor de ideas entre hombre y hombre" (IV, 1173). Manso further attributes his success with Manolo to having taught by examples: "En la esfera moral, la experiencia ha hecho más adeptos que los sermones, y la desgracia, más cristianos que el Catecismo" (IV, 1175).

Having finished his tutoring of Manolo, Manso is occupied in various services to the family of his wealthy brother, José María. Manso shows his awareness of the role he has assumed in his brother's family when he affirms: "La familia confiaba principalmente en mí, en mí rara bondad y en mi corazón humanitario" (IV, 1244).

In contrast to Manso, José María shows egotism in all of his behavior. Manso finds it necessary to defend Irene from the machinations of José María and doña Cándida. The professor learns that doña Cándida virtually holds Irene prisoner in a house rented and furnished by José María, who expects to "buy" her from her aunt. He also learns that José María comes often to the house to offer Irene gifts in exchange for his fawning love (IV, 1249). When Manso enters the house rented by José María, he sees Manolo and realizes that his former pupil and Irene have been seeing each other. After having foiled José María's project to seduce Irene, Manso comes to the realization that she and Manolo are in love. However, he is compensated by the feeling he has of having done well in protecting Irene—in having fulfilled his mission of service: "La energía moral, cierta robustez hercúlea que advertí en mí conciencia, dábanme fuerzas físicas, agilidad, actividad" (IV, 1264).[14] Before his death, Manso advises Manolo to marry Irene (IV, 1279). Shortly before his death, Manso expresses his recognition that his mission in life is to help others.

Contrasted with the ideal of individual service in *El amigo Manso* is the type of charity administered by organized groups. This type of charity is held up to ridicule by Manso. When José María sponsors a meeting of the *Sociedad para Socorro de los Inválidos* in his home, Manso ridicules the great number of committees and subcommittees organized to carry out the work of the Society. He always speaks of the group with irony: "¡Bienaventurados obreros, y que felices iban a ser cuando aquella máquina [the Society], todavía no armada, echase a andar, llenando a España con su admirable movimiento y esparciendo rayos de beneficencia por todas partes!"(IV, 1197). Later, Manso describes how the Society decides to spend the money it has accumulated:

Todo marchaba admirablemente, y marcharía mejor cuando los planes de los caritativos fundadores tuvieran completo desarrollo. Por de pronto, se había acordado destinar los cuantiosos fondos reunidos a imprimir los notabilísimos discursos que se pronunciaron en las turbulentas sesiones. ¡Lástima grande que tan admirable piezas de elocuencia se perdieran! (IV, 1207)

Called on to speak at a meeting of the Society to be held in the home of José María, Manso makes clear the reason for his aversion to giving this speech: "No han sido nunca de mi gusto estas ceremonias que con pretexto de un fin caritativo sirven para que exhiban multitud de tipos ávidos de notoriedad" (IV, 1224). Manso gives only the conclusions of his speech, and they are not particularly favorable to the view of organized charity as a social and economic instrument: "Mis conclusiones eran que los institutos oficiales de beneficencia no resuelven la cuestión del pauperismo sino en grado insignificante; que la iniciativa personal, que esas agrupaciones que se forman al calor de la idea cristiana . . . , en fin, mis conclusiones ofrecían escasa novedad y el lector sabe lo mismo que yo" (IV, 1231).

Manso's continuing care for doña Cándida's basic needs stems from the behest of his mother on her deathbed (IV, 1175). What makes doña Cándida's parasitism so particularly trying is the indirection with which she pursues it. Too proud to ask for help directly, she always brings a worthless article to Manso on the pretext of doing him a favor by selling it to him at a lower price than she could get elsewhere (IV, 1176–1178). Doña Cándida is a "flat" character. One of her functions in the novel is to reveal the depth and development of Manso's charitableness. In spite of his recognition of her crass materialism and in spite of his feeling of repugnance toward her, Manso continues to help her until the time of his death. While his position of having to advise Manolo as to whether or not he should marry Irene is the most intense test to which he must subject his ideal of service, his sustained charitableness toward the ubiquitous, wearisome doña Cándida attests his perseverance in remaining true to his ideal.

According to Galdós there were three religious institutions in Madrid for the correction of women at the time of the action in the novel (1869–1876) *Fortunata y Jacinta* (V, 237). They were all built by the collection of alms and furnished through donations of furniture (V, 229–237). One of these institutions, Las Micaelas, is the site of the action of a significant portion of the novel. There are two divisions in Las Micaelas: one for *filomenas,* women subject to correction, and the other for *josefinas,* young girls placed there by their parents or guardians to be educated by the nuns (V, 233). The novel is concerned only with the *filomenas.*

Library of

Davidson College

The first mention of Las Micaelas is made by Jacinta when she tells the sister of the alcoholic Mauricia, la Dura, that she is a friend of the nuns of Las Micaelas and has faith that they will cure her (v, 120). If Jacinta's faith in Las Micaelas is somewhat naive and misleading, the un-alloyed praise of the institution by the priest, Nicolás Rubín, should suffice to make the reader suspicious of its efficacy in reforming those who enter its doors (v, 217). Rubín advises Fortunata to enter Las Micaelas in order to assure her complete reform prior to her marriage with his brother, Maxi. During Fortunata's stay in Las Micaelas the scene of the action shifts to the institution.

At Las Micaelas the inculcation of Christian doctrine is considered adequate to equip the inmates to struggle with life outside the institution. Referring to their ignorance of the fundamental motives of Fortunata's behavior, and by inference the motives of the other inmates, Galdós makes this comment about the nuns of Las Micaelas: "Verdad que en todo lo que corresponde al reino inmenso de las pasiones, las monjas apenas ejercitaban su facultad educatriz, bien porque no conocieron aquel reino, bien porque se asustaron de asomarse a sus fronteras" (v, 248). There is a criticism here of the inadequacy of the education of the nuns themselves. Their faulty education could doubtless be traced back to the false assumptions of a dogmatic and narrow religion, but since Galdós does not develop this theme further in this novel, it is inappropriate to speculate further on the matter. Neither Fortunata nor Mauricia discloses in her subsequent behavior any change that is either directly or indirectly attributable to the influence of Las Micaelas.

In his novels Galdós reveals himself to be favorable to charity carried out by individuals rather than that organized by groups, but his approval depends partly upon the motives of the individual undertaking the charitable enterprise and partly upon the social consequences of such an enterprise.

In *La desheredada* (1881), when Muñoz y Nones, the father-in-law of Augusto Miquis, visits Isidora in jail to advise her to desist in her lawsuit to prove that she is the granddaughter of the marquesa de Aransis, he is described as having a "gran calva lustrosa, bajo la cual actuaba sin cesar el prurito de la fundación de una *Penitenciaría para jóvenes delincuentes"* (IV, 1140). At the end of the interview, he promises Isidora that her delinquent younger brother, Mariano, will be one of the first to be admitted when his institution is inaugurated (IV, 1143). Nothing more is said about Muñoz y Nones's project; it is known, however, that Mariano will never have the opportunity to benefit from it, since he is caught in an attempt to assassinate the king. It is probable that Galdós, in his account of the *penitenciaría* of Muñoz y Nones, wishes to point out the need for immediate concerted public action to remedy the conditions that produce juvenile delinquents, as well as the need to reform them, instead of leaving such an important matter in the hands of private individuals, who may or may not take action to alleviate the problem. What is certain is that Mariano, when he attempts the assassination of the king, proves that society is an organic entity and can ill afford to neglect any of its members.

Earlier, when Mariano, as a young boy, had gravely wounded one of his companions with a knife, the people of Madrid were in a furor because such an outrage could occur in their city. Committees and subcommittees were appointed to study the case, the press militantly advocated that something be done to prevent this from happening again, and orators took advantage of the incident to win an ephemeral popularity. The outcome of so much indignation is logical only if it is seen in the perspective given by Galdós:

> Tanta actividad, tanta charla, tanto proyecto de escuelas, de penitenciarías, de sistemas teóricos, prácticos, mixtos, sencillos y complejos, celulares, y panoscópicos, docentes y correcionales, fueron cayendo en el olvido, como los juguetes del niño, abandonados y rotos ante la ilusión del jugete nuevo. El juguete nuevo de aquellos días fué un proyecto urbano más práctico y, además esencialments burocrático. Ocupáronse de él juntas y comisiones, las cuales trabajaron tan bien y con tanto espíritu de realidad, que al poco tiempo se alzó grandiosa, provocativamente bella y monumental, todo roja y feroz, la nueva plaza de toros. (IV, 1010)

There is no guarantee, then, that if the public abdicates its responsibility to provide education for the poor and to resolve the problem of juvenile delinquency, the slack will be taken up by charitable individuals. Mariano is not, in fact, helped by either the one or the other—his lack of education is allowed to pursue its logical course until he attempts a crime of such far-reaching consequences that he must be removed from society.

The indefatigable charitable energy of the tough-minded, but tender-hearted doña Guillermina Pacheco in *Fortunata y Jacinta* is difficult to describe in few words. Doña Guillermina is persistent in her charitable endeavors, but her most characteristic trait is the intensity with which she pursues them.

Her principal occupation is an orphanage of some hundred children which she has founded and maintains through the diligent collection of alms (v, 77). Doña Guillermina is possessed of particularly suitable qualifications for organizing and supervising an orphanage; Galdós enumerates them: "No nació aquella sin igual mujer para la vida contemplativa. Era un temperamento soñador, activo y emprendedor; un espíritu con ideas propias y con iniciativas varoniles" (v, 76). The novelist then speaks of her "carácter inflexible," "facultades de organización," and "perseverancia grandiosa" (v, 76). Doña Guillermina withdrew her membership from a charitable association of aristocratic ladies in order to found an orphanage. Doña Guillermina's dedication to the orphanage makes her, by no means, remiss in other forms of charity: "Y a propio tiempo repartía periódicamente cuantiosas limosnas entre la gente pobre de los distritos de la Inclusa y Hospital; vestía a muchos niños, daba ropa a los viejos, medicinas a los enfermos y alimentos y socorros diversos a todos" (v, 76, 77).[15]

What makes doña Guillermina interesting and attractive is the humorous arrogance with which she importunes people—ranging from prostitutes to the king and queen in order to provide the necessities of life for her orphans (v, 77–78). She provides more than the necessities of life for them since she has two schools and a shoe shop in the house that serves as an orphanage. Her ambition is to erect a new building so that she can take care of two or three hundred children. To build the new orphanage, she wants not money but material. The reader is given a sample of the philanthropist's persuasive powers when, during an unexpected visit to don Baldomero Santa Cruz's home, she obtains from each of the guests a promise to donate specific items to her project (v, 78–79). She rarely appears with friends and relatives without badgering them for donations for the building (v, 128, 318, 320, 456). Particularly humorous is her relationship with her nephew, Manuel Moreno-Isla. Upon having been accosted by his aunt shortly after entering Spain, Moreno-Isla replies: "Apenas se pone el pie en España, no se da paso sin tropezar con bandoleros. Ahora pretende que entre todos los parientes le hagamos un piso" (v, 318).[16]

If the sincerity of doña Guillermina's charity is not sufficiently clear from the time and energy which she dedicates to the welfare of her orphanage and to the erection of a new building, then it should be evident from the help she gives to various other individuals in the novel.

One critic, in a study of doña Guillermina, has cited among other things evidence of Galdós's critical attitude toward organized charity in other novels, such as *Marianela,* to imply that the author also disapproves of doña Guillermina's charity.[17] The study made here reveals no evidence that Galdós disapproves of doña Guillermina's charitable activities. Although her methods of persuading people to give are sometimes overbearing, they are presented in a light that is humorous, not satirical, and they are shown to be natural. Furthermore, doña Guillermina's motives are never questioned or held up to ridicule and the reader is made to perceive the good results she engineers both for her orphanage and the individuals whom she helps. Whether or not the problem of the poor and orphaned is adequately resolved by doña Guillermina, she is able to alleviate some suffering.

Unlike doña Guillermina Jordana in *La loca de la casa* (1892) exhibits a great deal of servile indirection when asking for donations. Speaking of the wealthy Pepet Cruz, who has been the object of his attentions, Jordana himself unashamedly admits this: "Le alojo en mi casa, le colmo de atenciones, hasta le adulo . . . , con la esperanza de que costee la terminación de mi grandioso hospital . . . , y nada, no entiende mis indirectas" (v, 1625).[18] Jordana's adulation fails to make a dent in the materialistic armor of Cruz. Nevertheless, through persistence, the philanthropist learns of a weakness in that armor, in the love that he has for his charitable wife Victoria, and this gives him hope of eventually obtaining aid from the obdurate industrialist (v, 1663, 1671). Jordana's estimate of the power of Victoria over Cruz proves to be well-founded when she extracts from her husband, as a condition for the termination of their separation, the promise to finish the construction of the hospital and wing for the orphanage (v, 1674).

The humiliation Jordana is willing to endure in the pursuit of his charitable goals attests his real compassion. Were this insufficient evidence, then his ultimate success should suffice to indicate Galdós's approval of his charity, especially since Cruz's donations are symptomatic of a desirable change in his conduct—from the utter rejection of any form of giving to an external observance of charity.

Public Beneficence

Public beneficence refers to charitable institutions under the control and management of the government. It rarely becomes a focal theme in Galdós's novels, assuming importance in only two or three novels. It might seem strange that a realistic novelist such as Galdós, would neglect to present in depth such an important sphere of his social environment, but when it is realized that individuals and small groups often attempt to establish essentially the same type of institutions, the reasons become more apparent. Galdós's basic assumption that the effectiveness of an institution depends upon the people who comprise it, is more susceptible to novelistic elaboration through character studies of the individuals involved in the founding of charitable institutions than through the presentation of a governmental bureaucracy.

The description of the insane asylum at Leganés, with which *La desheredada* (1881) begins, reveals the various functions that the institution has in society: "allí es donde se ve todo el horror de esa sección espantosa de la Beneficencia, en que se reúnen la caridad cristiana y la defensa social, estableciendo una lúgubre fortaleza llamada manicomio, que, juntamente, es hospital y presidio!" (IV, 967).[19] The charitable treatment which the inmates receive comes from "las hermanas de la caridad, alma y sostén del asilo por estar encargadas de su régimen doméstico" (IV, 969). The necessity to make a prison of Leganés is made worse by the inhuman treatment the inmates receive at the hands of the guards. The novelist gives this description of them: "No hay compasión en su rostros, ni caridad en sus almas. De cuantos funcionarios ha podido inventar la tutela del Estado, ninguno es tan antipático como el domador de locos. El día en que la ley haga desparecer al verdugo, sería un día grande si al mismo tiempo la caridad hace desaparecer al loquero" (IV, 968). Galdós's criticism of the brutality of the guards implies that charity would be more appropriate in dealing with the inmates. However, his previous description of the egotism which prevails in the institution, when he says that "el egoismo ha llegado aquí a su grado máximo" (V, 968),[20] makes such a solution impractical since force would necessarily have to be used to restrain such selfishness. It is possible that Galdós intended to imply that the helpless inmates not only should be treated with compassion from the standpoint of Christian charity, but that charitable treatment would also provide an atmosphere in which they could improve their mental condition. The idea that love begets love, and hate begets hate is a fundamental assumption of Galdós's psychology of love. If the novelist did intend to advocate the solution of more charitable treatment of the inmates, then he partially defeated his purpose by overstressing their selfishness.

When Mariano Rufete, in *La desheredada,* gravely wounds one of his companions, the reactions of an official of *Beneficencia* and an alderman who happen to be passing by at the time, are significant. Galdós uses the words "¡Horror y escándalo!" to describe their feelings (IV, 1006). In other words they see the crime of Mariano, not as a natural consequence of the neglect of his education and upbringing amidst great poverty, but as an inexplicable occurrence demonstrating the boy's innate wickedness. The official of *Beneficencia* is for showing no mercy to Mariano when from his refuge in a sewer, the boy hits him on the head with a brick after being threatened by him (IV, 1007). The delinquent is finally lured into the arms of a member of the civil guard, who offers him two oranges (IV, 1010). Mariano's resentment of authority is such that he reacts to the threat of force with greater recalcitrance and is subdued only through kindness.

Galdós, then, approves of organized charity to the extent that it serves individual needs without humiliating or dehumanizing the recipient. Those who administer organized charity or public welfare in a way that degrades the recipient are invariably satirized. Galdós criticizes the values which led Spanish society to expend its material and human resources in producing luxuries, rather than applying these resources to correct the social injustices which organized charity seeks to alleviate.

Notes

[1] Eoff, *The Novels of Pérez Galdós* (1954), p. 90.

[2] "Sociology and Philanthropy," *Annals of the American Academy of Political and Social Science,* 12 (1898): 55.

[3] Galdós insists on this theme of social injustice in all of Jacinta's visits to the poor neighborhood; see also p. 119.

[4] v, 123, 125. An implicit belief in the necessity of being indulgent with the poor is evident in don Evaristo Feijoo's advice to Fortunata that she can only be relatively virtuous unless she goes back to her husband, since she has no decent way of making money to support herself (v, 331).

[5] In *Halma* it is partly Halma's financial aid to Urrea that enables him to reform his life (v, 1799, 1824).

[6] See *El doctor Centeno* (IV, 1363, 1409, 1449) for a further illustration of the relationship between excessive generosity and parasitism. In *Torquemada en el purgatorio* Torquemada justifies his miserliness by affirming that he will not be the one who subsidizes mendicancy (v, 1100).

[7] This same attitude toward the government is commented on later by Manolo Infante in *La incógnita* (v, 716, 720).

[8] See, for example, IV, 1709, 1716–1717, 1726, 1746, 1774.

[9] The idea of a struggle for existence in nature was one of the cornerstones of Charles Darwin's theory of evolution (published in *Origin of Species* in 1859). Those animals unable to adapt to their environment or unable to compete with the other animals perished, thereby leaving only the strong to reproduce themselves. Over the ages, this process tended to result in more vigorous individuals among the species which survived. For a discussion of how Darwin's theory was applied to economics, see Bertrand Russell, *A History of Western Philosophy* (1959), pp. 780–781. Friedrich

Nietzsche (1844–1900) saw in the Christian ethic of love, an attempt of the weak to dilute the natural and rightful power of the strong. See Russell, pp. 763–768. For a similar statement by Cruz in this novel, see v, 1640.

[10] A modern sociologist has come to essentially the same conclusion as Cruz. Edward Alsworth Ross in "Philanthropy from the Viewpoint of the Sociologist," Ellsworth Faris et al., eds., *Intelligent Philanthropy* (1930), says this: "The custom of giving something for nothing virtually puts a premium on that conduct, trait, or plight which enables one to qualify to receive alms. Once almsgiving is general and regular enough for the parasitic to count upon it, then, if being destitute qualifies one to claim alms, there are those who will idly drink up or squander or gamble away their resources trusting to the generosity of the charitable to extricate them from the inevitable consequences of such conduct" (p. 266).

[11] iv, 716. See also iv, 733, for Sofía's contemptuous treatment of Marianela.

[12] Golfín's cure of Pablo is based on both compassion and knowledge; see iv, 687, 690, 719. For further instances of his kindness toward Nela, see iv, 692, 694, 722, 742, 743, 750.

[13] Wines, p. 49. In *La familia de León Roch* mindless organized charity is implicitly attacked by Galdós on more than one occasion (iv, 797, 871, 824–825).

[14] For a further indication of Manso's feeling of having worked well here, see iv, 1264–1265. He exalts the beneficial influence of the individual conscience.

[15] For specific examples, see v, 102, 236, 363–364, 372, 382–383, 393, 519–525, 529–532.

[16] See also v, 79, 320, 401–403, 456.

[17] J. L. Brooks, "The Character of Doña Guillermina Pacheco in Galdós's Novel *Fortunata y Jacinta,*" *BHS,* 38 (1961): 87.

[18] See also v, 1647, 1648, 1664.

[19] Leganés is the institution to which Maxi Rubín is taken at the end of *Fortunata y Jacinta* (v, 547–548).

[20] See also v, 965–967.

III   Religious and Ethical Aspects of Charity

ALTHOUGH CRITICS have often commented on Galdós's attitude toward religion,[1] they have written with greater certitude when affirming the constant ethical concern revealed in his novels.[2] Galdós never makes his religious beliefs explicit in his novels; while he attacks certain negative tendencies of Spanish Catholicism, at the same time he extols certain positive ethical values, whether they be embodied in the conduct of ostensibly religious persons or not.

Galdós is revealed to be both traditional and modern in his view of charity: traditional in that he harks back to the primitive emphasis on adhering to the spirit of the command to "love thy neighbor as thyself" rather than to the mere letter; modern in that he breaks the theological crust that over the centuries has hardened this teaching into rigid religious dogma. Galdós values love as an emotion or a mental state rather than merely a principle.[3] The characters in his novels who practice charity out of duty rather than out of genuine feeling are held up to ridicule. Those who, by going through the motions of religious devotion and by giving alms, believe that they are demonstrating their love of God are considered by the novelist as hypocritical or superstitious. To say this is not to preclude authentic religious feeling in any of those characters who observe external religious practices; all sorts of combinations are found. A charitable disposition may be found in a religious person who observes external forms, in one who does not, and even in one who is apparently without religion. And it may not be found in persons fitting these three descriptions. As a general rule, however, those individuals who observe the external forms most noisily are those whose motives are most suspect.[4]

Galdós is also modern in that he avoids fitting his views on charity into a monolithic system of ideas, as thinkers have tended to do in the past. From his criticism of the tendency of the primitive Christian teachings on charity to harden into rules, it would follow logically that he would want to avoid setting up a system of ideas tantamount to instant petrifaction which would, furthermore, tend to separate men. Galdós's conception of charity as a fluid, flexible, elusive feeling requires that it be experienced through the nondiscursive form of the novel rather than conveyed through the discursive language of reason.[5]

If, as Unamuno claims, individualism is a peculiarly Spanish tradition,[6] then Galdós's novels lie within that tradition because of the preeminence which he gives to the individual conscience.[7] The novelist has faith that the conscience, though it appears to be an anarchical force, ultimately tends toward harmony. One of Galdós's assumptions about human beings is that they all need love and need to love others in order to maintain an integrated personality; if an individual fails to love, he receives warning signs in the form of neurotic or psychotic symptoms, or his conscience bothers him. In other words, the conscience is an instrument of restoring moral equilibrium if its messages are heeded. In some individuals the conscience is weak and underdeveloped; in others, it is highly creative and attains a quasi-mystical synthetic power. In such consciences love is given precedence over all other human relationships. Little else seems to matter. Galdós's portrayal of these individuals reveals his attitude toward charity in its most positive form.

Galdós's emphasis on the religious and ethical aspects of love changed in the course of his novelistic career. The *Novelas de la primera época* are filled with hate and destructive religious forces, whereas novels such as *Nazarín* (1895), *Halma* (1895), and *Misericordia* (1897), written at the height of his novelistic powers, emphasize the positive ethic of love. W. H. Shoemaker, in an article entitled "Cara y cruz de la novelística galdosiana," has compared *Doña Perfecta* (1876) and *Misericordia* (1897), revealing among other things how the two novels respectively epitomize Galdós's negative emphasis on the theme of religion in his early novels and his positive emphasis on this theme in the novels of his maturity.[8]

Charity as Duty versus Charity as Emotion

Galdós invariably satirizes those characters who accompany the charitable acts which they perform with remarks that it is their Christian duty to be charitable. Their conduct is not considered charitable; true charity is effusive and spontaneous and comes from the heart.

When a ship is wrecked near Ficóbriga in *Gloria* (1876–1877), the principal citizen of the town, don Juan Lantigua takes Daniel Morton, one of the survivors, into his home. Lantigua emphasizes to the Jew Daniel Morton that such charity is within the framework of Christian duty. He says: "Dios nos manda consolar al triste, amparar al desvalido," and then reiterates that they are bound by duty to help Daniel: "Es lo más sencillo y fácil que nos ha mandado Jesucristo" (IV, 537).

When at a religious banquet, it is mentioned that Daniel is a Jew, the priest, don Silvestre, who had saved Daniel's life, is obviously filled with chagrin at having saved a Jew. He feels now that he must justify his charitable act on the basis of duty: "A pesar de eso, no me pesa haberle salvado la vida—dijo con petulancia don Silvestre—, porque está escrito: 'Bendecid a los que os maldicen y haced bien a los que os aborrecen" (IV, 586).

The usurer, Juan Amarillo, helps Daniel find a place to stay in Ficóbriga because he is impressed by the Jew's wealth. He justifies this service with this bit of hypocrisy: "nada perdía nuestra santa religión porque se diese posada al peregrino, y que la doctrina evangélica prescribía hacer bien a los enemigos" (IV, 626).

Set against this ritualistic charity is the spontaneous charity practiced out of real compassion by Daniel. Although Daniel tells Gloria that his religion advocates the practice of charity (IV, 581), there is no indication that his charity is anything other than spontaneous. The generosity of Daniel reveals that charitable individuals are found in all religions. Moreover, charity born of authentic compassion rather than of a sense of duty is desirable whatever the religion of the benefactor may be.

In *El abuelo* (1897) Venancio and Gregoria, the former tenants and servants of the impoverished conde de Albrit, find it difficult to fulfill their Christian duty of being charitable to the aged, arrogant aristocrat when he returns to the house that once was his, but now is in their hands. The conde has returned to his old home to verify which of the two girls who pass as his granddaughters is the real one, since one of them is illegitimate. The two girls are living temporarily at the old homestead with Venancio and Gregoria. Prior to Albrit's arrival, Venancio makes this rejoinder to his wife's assertion that they have to help the conde: "Claro; le ampararemos, le socorreremos. Ha sido nuestro señor, nuestro amo; en su casa hemos comido, hemos trabajado . . . Pues sí hay aquí cristianismo, delicadeza" (VI, 13–14). It is obvious from the last sentence that Venancio is assuming the role of a Christian who is punctilious in observing all of his duties. The conde, who because of his habit of command and his blindness has grown more arrogant and hard to please in his old age, remembers the time when he was generous with Venancio and Gregoria, and they responded with affection and veneration (VI, 26).

The first test of the charity of Venancio and Gregoria comes when the conde insists on occupying an upstairs room used to store beans. Instead of delicately complying with the conde's desire by moving the beans to another room, Venancio stubbornly resists (VI, 26–27). The couple then begins to complain of the conde shortly after this conflict, and suggests to the priest and doctor, whose education, incidentally, was paid for by the conde, that he would be better off somewhere else. Together, they conspire to send him to a monastery nearby (VI, 50–51, 66, 77–83), but the scheme fails when the indignant conde refuses to stay in the monastery (VI, 82–83). Meanwhile, Venancio and Gregoria's abuses continue.

The conde finally becomes so angered by such treatment

that he is provoked to launch a verbal attack on Venancio and Gregoria, making explicit their failure to fulfill their Christian duty to be kind to him, not to mention their incapacity for heartfelt love:

> No tenéis ni un destello de generosidad en vuestras almas ennegrecidas por la avaricia; no sois cristianos; no sois nobles, que también los de origen humilde saben serlo; no sois delicados, porque en vez de dar un consuelo a mi grandeza caída, la pisoteáis; vosotros que en el calor de mi casa pasasteis de animales a personas. Sois ricos . . . ; pero no sabéis serlo. (VI, 72)

The resolve of Venancio and Gregoria to fulfill their Christian duty proves to be very fragile, because there is no real kindness underneath.

Love and Dogma

As Balseiro has pointed out, Galdós "odiaba cuanto tiende a separar por puntos de doctrina a los hombres, que deben unirse por naturaleza y amor."[9] Religious precepts, which in a confusion of means and ends have been hardened into dogmas more important than the human beings they are supposed to serve, are often the object of Galdós's criticism, especially in his earlier novels. He attacks religion so rigidly conceived as to be stifling to all that is natural and expansive in life. He attacks such religion because it is based on a negative approach to life; it is a dogmatic religion based on what Bertrand Russell calls "taboo ethics"—a series of "thou shalt nots."[10] Galdós implies a criticism of the concept of sin which is revealed so often to be the springboard from which certain individuals in his novels launch cruel destructive offensives against their fellow man. Whether these assaults have as their object the active destruction of the person considered to be wicked (according to a preconceived conviction as to what constitutes sin) or whether the object is to reform the wicked person, the result is the same: destruction. Dogmatic religion too frequently places in the hands of people, who for diverse reasons tend to be cruel, an instrument for disrupting the lives of those who violate religious taboos.

The effects of religious intolerance on the lives of the young engineer Pepe Rey and Rosario Polentinos in *Doña Perfecta* (1876) have been described in an earlier chapter. The two characters who represent that religious intolerance are doña Perfecta, Pepe's aunt and the mother of Rosario, and don Inocencio, a priest.

Don Inocencio, in his first encounter with Pepe, provokes the engineer to such a vehement defense of his liberal views that he arouses the doubts of his reactionary aunt as to his belief in God (IV, 421–424). So narrow are the religious beliefs of don Inocencio and doña Perfecta that they take Pepe's liberal views as atheism. In a conversation with his niece, María Remedios, who is ambitious for her own son to marry Rosario, the priest explains his attitude toward Pepe: "como director espiritual de la casa, debía tomar cartas en el asunto, y las tomé. Ya sabes que le puse la proa como vulgarmente se dice. Desenmascaré sus vicios; descubrí su ateísmo; puse a la vista de todo el mundo la podredumbre de aquel corazón materializado" (IV, 486). Don Inocencio goes on to tell how he suggested various subtle underhanded stratagems to doña Perfecta to separate Pepe from Rosario and cause him to leave Orbajosa (IV, 486–487).

The priest finds doña Perfecta an apt pupil in matters of clandestine persecution; in fact, the pupil exceeds the teachings of her master. Doña Perfecta, in the face of Pepe's persistent efforts to see Rosario, abandons the subtle methods of persuasion suggested by don Inocencio and orders her nephew shot when he is discovered in her orchard one night. Rosario has to be committed to an insane asylum after this occurrence.

Doña Perfecta justifies her persecution of her nephew on religious grounds. Once she assumes that Pepe is an atheist, she feels free to use any means to separate him from her daughter (IV, 464). At the end of the novel, Galdós makes explicit the religious origin of doña Perfecta's cruelty toward Pepe and Rosario:

No sabemos como hubiera sido doña Perfecta amando. Aborreciendo, tenía la inflamada vehemencia de un ángel tutelar de la discordia entre los hombres. Tal es el resultado producido en un carácter duro y sin bondad nativo por la exaltación religiosa, cuando ésta, en vez de nutrirse de la conciencia y de la verdad revelada en principios tan sencillos como hermosos, busca su savia en fórmulas estrechas que sólo obedecen a intereses eclesiásticos. Para que la mojigatería sea inofensiva, es preciso que exista en corazones muy puros. Es verdad que aún en este caso es infecunda para el bien. (IV, 496)

Note that Galdós is attributing a negative effect only to dogmatic religion, not to religion as such. Furthermore, he indicates that adherence to religion based on dogma nullifies any positive influence that the "pure in heart" might have.

The conduct of members of both the Christian and Jewish faiths in *Gloria* leads to the conclusion that creedal dogmatism in any religion is deleterious to the growth of love.[11] During his convalescence, Daniel and Gloria, the daughter of don Juan, fall in love with each other. Since Daniel is a Jew and Gloria a Christian, they part when Daniel is well enough to leave, agreeing that marriage is impossible unless one of them is willing to convert to the other's religion—a sacrifice neither is prepared to make. Daniel sees Gloria again, however, when circumstances force him to return temporarily to Ficóbriga. On this occasion he is discovered alone in the house with Gloria by don Juan. He is so horrified that he is struck dead with apoplexy. Daniel leaves, but returns later when he learns that Gloria has had a child by him. When out of charity toward Gloria, Daniel pretends to have converted to Christianity so that she will agree to marry him, his mother, an intransigent Jewess, exposes her son's plan and unscrupulously forces him to return to his home in England. Gloria dies as a result of these events, while Daniel is reported to have lost him mind searching for a universal religion. The child Jesús remains as the only fruit of their love.

The intensity of religious dogmatism exists in varying degrees in the characters of *Gloria*. Don Juan Lantigua's observance of charity as a Christian duty has already been discussed above. Don Juan is a man who is inflexible in both his feelings and his ideas (IV, 509). Daniel is cared for in his home out of a sense of Christian duty (IV, 531). It is partly because of the pressure exerted by don Juan on his daughter to give up her liberal ideas on religion that a deeper chasm is created between Daniel and Gloria. When Gloria feels her liberal ideas adversely affecting her relations with her father and his brother, the bishop don Angel, she resolves to rid herself of these ideas: "¡Ay! Quién puede resistir a tanta autoridad ni a tanta bondad? Me declaro conquistada. Creo todo lo que la Santa Madre Iglesia nos manda creer" (IV, 567). Before it was known that he was a Jew, Daniel was treated as befits an individual in distress; he is now avoided.

Don Juan's brother, don Angel, is depicted as having a great deal of spontaneous good will toward his fellow man (IV, 519). He was kind to Gloria as a child and reveals a tolerant solicitude for her as a young lady (IV, 515-516). Furthermore, the charity which he advocates and practices is manifestly heartfelt (IV, 533, 552). In spite of the goodness of don Angel's intention, his imposition of his religious ideas on Gloria does her a great deal of harm. Like don Juan, he uses his authority to exert pressure on Gloria to reject her tolerant ideas. When Gloria confesses to her uncle her love of Daniel and her belief that Daniel will be saved, he replies that she has been contaminated with "latitudinarismo" and must stifle her love for him with the love of God (IV, 565). Love of God, as he conceives it, precludes human love between certain individuals. Gloria's first impulse is to rely on her own intelligence and rebel against her uncle's advice to be intolerant, but his authority and the esteem in which she holds him, finally wears down her resistance (IV, 566). Later, when don Angel observes his brother lying prostrate upon the floor as a result of having found Daniel and Gloria alone in his house, his deepest feelings of intolerance toward the Jew, whom he has unsuccessfully attempted to convert (IV, 547), surge to the surface as he snaps at Daniel: "¡Deicida, sal de aquí!" (IV, 581). With this epithet, he reveals not only how religious ideas have interfered with his own natural goodness, but also he reflects the traditional Catholic intolerance toward Jews.

The chapter describing the banquet celebrating the political victory of the forces of God, the political party of the priest, Silvestre Romero and the lawyer, Rafael del Horro, is ironically entitled "Agape" (a primitive Christian love feast). Instead of love ruling, however, many speeches are made advocating war against the enemies of Christianity. The

God invoked is the Old Testament God of wrath rather than the New Testament God of love (IV, 572). Don Juan Lantigua criticizes the warlike attitude of those present at the banquet when he says this: "Se habla mucho de batallar y poco del amor de Dios" (IV, 573). However, he reveals himself to be very intolerant later when as a preface to attacking the Protestant Reformation and rationalism, he makes this assertion: "Gozaba España desde edades remotas el inestimable beneficio de poseer la única fe verdadera, sin mezcla de otra creencia alguna ni de sectas bastardas" (IV, 573). Such assumptions as this led to the organization of the Counter Reformation. Galdós seems to recreate this atmosphere of religious militancy with this historical precedent in mind.

The intolerant atmosphere created by this religious exclusivism is revealed in the treatment Daniel receives when he returns to Ficóbriga after learning of the birth of his and Gloria's child. He is held prisoner temporarily, is the object of verbal abuse on the street, and is refused lodging (IV, 609–610). The tavernkeeper who refuses him lodging will only give him a little food. And when Daniel gives a blind beggar some money, the man hurls it to the ground, recognizing Daniel by the generosity of the alms: "Tome usted sus doblones, que ningún cristiano recibe el dinero por que fue vendido el Señor" (IV, 611). Daniel must suffer further insult at the hands of the sexton, Caifás, who has reason to be grateful since Daniel had given him money to pay his debts in time of great need. He offers Daniel lodging, but refuses to help him in any other way. Furthermore, he tells Daniel that the priest to whom he confesses has advised him to return the money that he has been given by the Jew (IV, 613–614).

Perhaps the greatest suffering which Gloria undergoes after the birth of her child is the humiliation inflicted upon her by her aunt, Serafina de Lantigua. Though it is unconscious, the aunt's cruelty to Gloria takes the form of interpreting the birth of her child within the framework of a narrowly conceived religion. Serafina's goal is to persuade Gloria to leave her child and dedicate herself to God in a convent. To accomplish this goal, Serafina tries to make Gloria conscious of the enormity of her sin, thereby causing the young woman great anguish. On one occasion, she tells Gloria of the reluctance of certain women to use the flowers which she had contributed for the procession of Holy Week (IV, 602). Gloria replies that she forgives them and admits that her guilt is great, but that she is willing to suffer. Serafina wants nothing less than her renunciation of her personality: "Padeces, sí, padeces—dijo la tía con amor—, pero no lo bastante. Hay en tu mismo martirio y en la expiación de que hables una independencia, una nueva rebeldía, que ya es un nuevo pecado" (IV, 603). Gloria's strongest tie to life is her son, and it is this tie that the childless Serafina would like to break: "Pero no basta crucificarte como mujer, sino como madre" (IV, 638).

Toward the end of the novel, Galdós reiterates that Serafina's cruelty is not conscious, but the result of her twisted interpretation of love of God. When she falls from weakness as a result of fasts while preparing Gloria's lunch the novelist exclaims: "¡Lástima grande que aquella santidad no fuese más humana!" (IV, 643).

In addition to Gloria and Daniel's inability to reconcile their religious differences, it is the religious fanaticism of Daniel's mother which intensifies the theme of religious intolerance. She comes to Ficóbriga with the express intention of preventing Daniel's marriage with Gloria. Berating Daniel for having forgotten the teachings of his religion, she exclaims: "un hijo mío morirá cien veces antes que arrodillarse delante de un sacerdote cristiano, y español por añadidura, y proclamar al mismo Cristo en la misma tierra que impíamente nos echó de sí, como a seres inmundos" (IV, 658). Daniel's confession that he is really going to remain true to his religion, even though married to a Christian, fails to mollify his mother. On the day of the wedding, she arranges for him to be arrested on the pretext that he stole money from his father before leaving England. The arrest is made in the most humiliating circumstances, in the presence of all the Lantigua family. The incredulous Daniel had not realized the extreme to which his mother's religious fanaticism would lead her (IV, 667). Like doña Perfecta, she considers any means legitimate to preserve the religious purity of her family.

Although the efforts of another of Gloria's uncles, the liberal don Buenaventura de Lantigua, to arrange the marriage between Daniel and his niece fail, he has the additional important functions in the novel of expressing pertinent criticism of a dogma-bound religion and serving as a foil, because of his tolerance, to many of the other characters. Discussing religion with Daniel, don Buenaventura says this:

> Yo creo que los hombres buenos y caritativos pueden salvarse, y se salvarán fácilmente, cualquiera que sea su religión. Creo que muchas cosas establecidas por la Iglesia, lejos de acrecentar la fe, la disminuyen, y que en todas las religiones, y principalmente a la nuestra, sobran reglas, disposiciones, prácticas. Creo que los cultos subsistirían mejor si volvieran a la sencillez primitiva. . . . Creo, finalmente, y para decirlo todo de una vez, que el fondo moral es con corta diferencia uno mismo en las religiones civilizadas . . . ; mejor dicho, que el hombre culto educado en la sociedad europea es capaz del superior bien, cualquiera que sea el nombre con que invoque a Dios. (IV, 617)

That don Buenaventura's words express the feelings of Galdós is borne out by the action of the novel itself. Charitableness is revealed in both Jews and Christians, while dogma creates an artificial separation between these two groups and hinders harmonious relations and the growth of love.

The true charity of the free thinker León Roch in *La familia de León Roch* is contrasted with the destructive religiosity of the Tellerías, his wife's family and Paoletti, the priest who is his wife's spiritual director. Neither the Tellerías nor Father Paoletti is able to conceive of charitableness outside of his narrowly focused view of Christianity. Gustavo admits the virtues of León, but attributes them to the desire to get on well in the words: "cumples ciertos preceptos por la razón sencilla de que es *cómodo ser bueno,* y porque el cumplimiento de los deberes externos siempre trae ventajas al individuo" (IV, 792).

When the survival of his estranged wife, María, depends upon convincing her that he still loves her, León, without hesitation, tells her the charitable lie she needs to hear (IV, 893–894). Paoletti balks, however, when León, motivated by pity, tries to persuade him of the necessity of maintaining the illusion that he loves María in order to keep her alive (IV, 900–901). The priest acquiesces to León's request, promising to use prudence, but not before revealing to the reader that he vacillates between an inflexible desire to adhere to the truth and León's charitable plea that he help save María's life (IV, 900–901).

León is proven to be right in his estimate of the harm that would be done to María's health by telling her the truth. After Gustavo tells her the truth, she has a relapse which ends with her death (IV, 925–926). Paoletti hastens María's death by telling her that León had demanded that Pepa Fúcar, the woman he loves, leave for appearance's sake, not because her presence would be painful to her (IV, 927). Paoletti also reveals here his assumption that a freethinker is incapable of charity. León proves the sincerity of his charity, when, after María's death he separates himself from Pepa permanently in order not to dishonor her and thereby spoil the future happiness of her daughter Monina, whom he also loves very much (IV, 956).

While the charitableness of León is considered by the Tellerías as hypocritical, the sterile self-sacrifice of María's brother, Luis Gonzaga, who is a monk, is considered virtuous (IV, 811). Luis feels so strongly that his brother-in-law is wicked that he feels authorized to advise María against any compromise with León on religious matters: "Entre él y tú no puede haber jamás sino la unión exterior, y vuestras almas estarán separadas por los abismos que hay entre el creer y no creer. Amor verdadero de esposos no puede existir entre vosotros. . . . No permitas que tu conciencia católica sea esclava de su arbitrariedad atea" (IV, 818). The atheism is a supposition on the part of Luis, based on León's religious skepticism and failure to observe the external forms of religion. María's decision to heed the advice of her brother eventually results in making her marriage with León intolerable, and leads to their separation. León, who has overheard Luis's advice to María, dreams that he kills a rigid insectlike being representing Luis and that he says this to him: "¿De dónde has venido con tu horrible orgullo disfrazado de virtud? . . . ¿De qué te vale el desollarte vivo, si no tienes verdadero espíritu de caridad?" (IV, 821).

Father Paoletti, like Nicolás Rubín in *Fortunata y Jacinta,* feels particularly qualified to offer advice on matters of love precisely because he himself is incapable of sexual love (IV, 911). Consequently, he advises María to purify herself of all love for León and is perplexed when she is unable to do so (IV, 927, 928, 930). His inability to feel human love makes him underestimate its power and overemphasize divine love. For this reason, he would have preferred to tell María the cruel truth that León no longer loved her, rather than save her life with a charitable lie.

External Devotion as Love of God

Certain characters in Galdós's novels, when they have gone through the motions of external religious devotion, feel that they have fulfilled their obligation to love God. For Galdós love of one's neighbor is inseparable from love of God; hence these characters are satirized. They adhere to the letter rather than to the spirit of the law. In the case of doña Guillermina Pacheco this is overstated, since she adheres to both the letter and the spirit, although Galdós does imply a criticism of her emphasis on observing rites.

The sister of don Juan de Moncada, doña Eulalia, is described in *La loca de la casa* (1892) as a person who spends her time praying, giving advice and expressing unfavorable opinions of everyone else (V, 1617). Eulalia tells Moncada that his troubles have their origin in his neglect of religious devotion: she warns him that his charitableness is not enough (V, 1621). Later, following her own advice, Eulalia refuses the request of her brother to help the indigent marquesa de Malavella. Instead, she hypocritically implies that she has no money and launches into a tirade against the poor marquesa. Before finishing, she also attacks Cruz for his materialism, Victoria for her apparent inability to change Cruz, and Moncada himself for adhering only to what she calls "exterioridades" of religion (V, 1651). The crowning ironic touch comes when, at the end of the scene with Moncada, the callous Eulalia self-righteously exclaims to her brother: "Piensa que somos sólo materia; que tenemos un espíritu" (v, 1652).

In the modesty with which she practices charitable acts, Rosaura, the wife of doña Juana Samaniego's nephew in *Casandra* (1905), is a foil to the embittered widow. Galdós makes this clear in an early description of the devoted mother of ten children: "Su modestia no da publicidad a sus virtudes, más excelsas por ser inconscientes, luminosas, tan sólo en la oscuridad" (vi, 125). In spite of the skimpy aid which doña Juana gives her family, Rosaura's attitude toward her is one of resignation and sincere good will (vi, 126). She befriends and aids Casandra despite the comments of other relatives and the possibility of alienating doña Juana, because she considers the young woman needful of friendship (vi, 133, 134). It is Rosaura, along with her husband, who arranges for the marriage in jail of Casandra and Rogelio (vi, 208). When Casandra almost idolizes Rosaura for so consoling her, her benefactor protests that she is unaware of having made any sacrifice (vi, 219). In the conversation between these two women which closes the novel, Casandra makes an assertion which obviously applies to doña Juana: "Demasiado ruido hace en el mundo la devoción para que sea de ley" (vi, 219). Rosaura's reply undoubtedly reflects Galdós's view: "La piedad verdadera florece en el silencio" (vi, 219).

Superstitious Charity

Galdós's characters often practice charity or offer prayers, believing that these acts will result in a favorable supernatural intervention in their lives, or that it will facilitate their entrance into heaven when they die. Such is the case with the marqués de Fúcar in *La familia de León Roch* (1878). When María, Leon Roch's wife is dying, the marqués, in whose house she is being attended, orders that masses be said for her every morning in his chapel. Galdós suggests that there is an ulterior motive (iv, 895). It is learned later that the marqués has received news of the return to Spain of his worthless son-in-law, who was assumed to have perished in a shipwreck (IV, 938–939). He hopes for some sort of supernatural liberation from the presence of his son-in-law in return for the masses.

In *Torquemada en la hoguera* (1889) Francisco Torquemada is described as a man who has amassed a small fortune through usury and the rental of houses. The debtors and tenants unable to meet their payments on time are mercilessly stripped of whatever material possessions they may have and are often left without money to buy food. Torquemada is completely devoid of compassion for those who fall in arrears in their payments (v, 906).

Torquemada's principal saving grace is his love for his twelve-year-old son, Valentín, who is a prodigy in mathematics. The father is inordinately proud of the boy (v, 910–912). When Valentín falls prey to illness, the desperate father, fearful of losing his son concludes that God is punishing him for his neglect of charity. The following Sunday he shocks his tenants by refusing to press them if they do not have the rent money. He praises his own charitableness and lectures them on the necessity of doing good to mankind since they will have to pay sooner or later for having neglected their fellow man's needs (v, 916–918). He also gives alms to a jobless man explaining that he had not given him anything on meeting him a few nights before because he was in a hurry (v, 920).

When Valentín shows improvement, Torquemada feels that he is on the right track in his newly acquired practice of charity. To his daughter's suggestion that he pray to the *Virgen del Carmen,* he replies: "Pero te advierto que no habiendo buenas obras no hay que fiarse de la Virgen. Y acciones cristianas habrá, cueste lo que cueste: yo te aseguro. En las obras de misericordia está todo el intríngulis. Yo vestiré enfermos, consolaré tristes . . . Bien sabe Dios que ésa es mi voluntad, bien lo sabe" (v, 921).

Torquemada's new charitableness is not completely unrestrained. On seeing a beggar one night who needs a coat, he hastens by him because he is wearing his new cloak. On arriving at his house he regrets having missed that opportunity. Changing to his old cloak, he goes out again and gives it to the beggar (v, 921–922). His habit of self-interest is also visible in his offer of a loan to Isidora Rufete and her consumptive husband, who paints for a living. After hesitating, he decides to make a gift of the three thousand *reales* which Isidora needs; but upon further reflection, he accepts Isidora's offer of some paintings and takes four of them (v, 929–930).

Valentín seems to have improved more when he returns home, so the usurer decides to ply the *Virgen del Carmen* with the gift of a pearl in order to reinforce the aid his son receives from supernatural sources. Tía Roma, his ancient maid, scoffs at the idea, telling him it would be better to sell the pearl and give the money to the poor (v, 931). Tía Roma energetically refuses a mattress which Torquemada tries to give her, since, as she says, the usurer's ideas are probably in the mattress and might contaminate her. She then leaves Torquemada dumbfounded by exposing the hypocrisy of his recent alms giving, reminding him of his past life full of petty stinginess and abuse of his wife, whom he nearly starved to death (v, 932–933).

Upon the death of Valentín, Torquemada is found embitteredly reverting to his old habits. He decides that a sum of money which he was going to use to help "cuatro pillos" will be better employed in giving his son a fine burial. His final words in this little novel, which are incidentally addressed to Tía Roma, reveal his bitter disillusionment at the failure of his superstitious hopes to be realized: "Ya sé que me vas a salir con el materialismo de la misericordia . . . A eso te respondo que si buenos memoriales eché, buenas calabazas me dieron. La misericordia que yo tengo, ¡puñales!, que me la claven en la frente" (v, 936).

The efforts of the priest, Pedro Gamborena, in *Torquemada y San Pedro,* to save the soul of Torquemada by converting him to a sincere feeling of charity toward his fellow man are made difficult because of the financier's longstanding habit of always seeking a return for his investments in the business world. When Torquemada tells Gamborena about his futile charity in behalf of Valentín, the priest replies: "La caridad debe practicarse siempre y por sistema—dijo el clérigo con severidad dulce—, no en determinados casos de apuro, como quien pone dinero a la lotería con avidez de sacar ganancia. Ni se debe hacer el bien por cálculo, ni el cielo es un ministerio al cual se dirigen memoriales para alcanzar un destino" (v, 1158).

These words seem not to have penetrated the mind of Torquemada, however, since he says later that he has nothing to confess to the priest. When Gamborena points out his avarice, Torquemada rejoins that the good which he has done for the government should be considered charity (v, 1177). Torquemada does promise to donate money to a hospital and help the poor when Gamborena frightens him with the prospect of hell.[12] He also agrees to give one-third of his wealth to the church provided he is saved; he pleads for his sister-in-law's assurance that God is good (v, 1182–1183). Torquemada feels much better after agreeing to give a third of his wealth to the church and even thinks that he will recover completely. He hints at changing his will should this happen, then contradicts himself with this utterance, indicating that he has conceived of his prospective donation as a business deal with God: "Soy hombre de palabra; y cuando digo: '¡Hecho!' la operación queda cerrada. No, no quiero en manera alguna romper mis buenas relaciones con el señor Dios, que tan bien se ha portado conmigo" (v, 1187). The following day, when the ailing miser has a relapse, he says that he is going to reduce the amount that he will give to the church to a prudent sum (v, 1191). After Gamborena tells him that his death is imminent and irremediable, Torquemada's utterances are too incoherent to determine if he has had a real change of heart (v, 1193–1196). What is certain is that up until this time he has considered his charity as a means of prying open the gates of heaven.

Humanitarian Charity

My concern here is with charity which is broadly based on religious principles—specifically those of primitive Christianity—yet which is humanitarian in its emphasis. This means that the well-being of the individual here on earth is considered important as well as his preparation for the life to come. Man is considered as something more than just a transient in this world; he is also conceived of as an end

64

within himself. Those, like Galdós, who so conceive man give importance to the individual conscience, while the significance attached to the formal trappings accreted to Christ's primitive teachings is minimized.

In *Angel Guerra* even though the religious fervor of Angel is a sublimation of his love for the nun, Leré, his growth toward greater love for his fellow man is real. Consequently, the plans which Angel has for establishing a series of charitable institutions based on the teachings of Christ should be seriously considered as possibly reflecting the viewpoint of Galdós himself of the need for widespread reform of religious institutions.

As Angel's spiritual inspiration, Leré sets him an example of active service; she belongs to one of those orders whose members go from house to house to collect alms to care for the sick, the aged, and the invalid (v, 1324–1325). Don Francisco Mancebo, a priest and the uncle of Leré's mother, has taken care of her family for a long time, and is opposed to this new type of order; he prefers that nuns remain in the cloister praying (v, 1324–1325). Thus tension between the traditional view of the function of religious orders and the modern view, whereby their members actively participate in alleviating social ills, is set up early in the respective religious careers of Angel and Leré. Angel is pleased with Leré's integration into the everyday world: "Leré no hablaba de cosas de fe si de ello no se le hablaba; no hacía pinitos de perfección; no se quejaba de su marcada discrepancia con el mundo presente, y hablaba y discurría como si todo cuanto la rodeaba estuviese en completa conformidad con ella" (v, 1341). Yet Leré reveals the strength of her religion when she is able to remain serene in the face of calumny to the effect that sexual attraction exists between Angel and her. Her only concern is to have a pure conscience (v, 1421).

Angel's plans to use his wealth to establish a charitable institution are unorthodox from the beginning. He tells the alcoholic don Pito that he will not have to stop drinking just because he will be taken care of by him: "Pero para todo hay bula compañero, y no estoy porque se condenen en absoluto los hábitos arraigados en una larga vida, y que al fin de ella vienen a ser la única alegría del anciano" (v,

1425). Angel conceives of don Pito as a sick man, not a sinner: "Vió a don Pito como un caso admirable para ejercer las obras de misericordia, un enfermo que necesitaba asistencia, y nada más" (v, 1429).

Angel later explains to Juan Casado, the priest who is his spiritual guide, the revolutionary nature of his charitable enterprises. In the first place, he wishes to take away the initiative from foreign countries in the building of modern orders in Spain (v, 1472). Angel will pay for the cost of the building and will maintain the order for a few years, and though he will admit alms and donations, no legacies or testamentary donations will be accepted (v, 1470). Angel goes on to explain to Casado his desire to follow the teachings of Christ in their purest form:

> En lo esencial quiero parecerme a los primitivos fundadores y seguir fielmente la doctrina pura de Cristo. Amparar al desvalido, sea quien fuere; hacer bien a nuestros enemigos, emplear siempre el cariño y la persuasión, nunca la violencia; practicar las obras de misericordia en espíritu y en letra sin distingos ni atenuaciones, y por fin, reducir el culto a las formas más sencillas dentro de la rúbrica. (v, 1471)

While Angel's plan to house men and women in the same building may be partly motivated by his love for Leré, the reasons which he adduces for this are fundamentally sound:

> La noción primera del amor no surge sino en medio de la vida, en el inmenso escenario poblado de seres distintos, y en el tumulto de las varias pasiones que los unen y los separan. Tanta reja, tanta precaución y tanto encierro entre paredes extinguen la fuente del amor. En cambio, el trato social y la castidad misma, aunque extraño parezca, la enriquecen de aguas purísimas. (v, 1477)

From these passages, it may be inferred that Angel wishes to avoid the creation of an institution such as Las Micaelas, whose inmates are expected to break long-standing habits immediately upon their entrance into the institution, and where knowledge of Christian doctrine is considered all that is necessary to cope with life outside.

Angel envisions a sweeping reform of traditional religious orders so that they may become more useful in alleviating social misery. After criticizing the church because "no practica la caridad más que en la parte que le conviene, para sostener su organización temporal" (v, 1514). Angel explains to Casado the idea behind this humanitarian charity: "El espiritualismo encarnado en las materialidades de la existencia, pues si Dios se hizo hombre, su doctrina tiene que hacerse Sociedad" (v, 1514). Angel's untimely death precludes his putting into effect his revolutionary plans; he renounces them as chimerical illusions, but the great amount of space and attention (v, 1531) which Galdós gives to these ideas indicates that there is a serious intention of social criticism, underlying their elaboration—criticism of the sterility of the traditional religious orders in Spain, and indication that they should be reformed and given a humanitarian basis.

The words and deeds of the priest in *Nazarín* (1895) disclosed how love of God is inseparable from love of man. Nazarín reveals that to attain this love the individual should follow the teachings of Christ and imitate him, relying on his own conscience to guide him rather than civil or ecclesiastical authority. Nazarín meets with resignation the harm that befalls him at the hands of both individuals and institutional authorities.

Motivated partly by the desire to avoid arrest for having cared for and lodged Andara (a woman who had begun a fight in a tavern and burned down a house), partly because of the eminent revocation of his permit to perform the duties of a priest, and partly because of his desire to get away from the corruption of the city, Nazarín leaves Madrid to wander about the countryside doing whatever good he can find to do and sustaining himself by begging for alms or taking whatever food is offered him. Andara and Beatriz, a prostitute who witnessed what she considered to be the miraculous cure by Nazarín of a baby, accompany him in his peregrination. The three walk from town to town performing various acts of charity, including burying and caring for the victims of a smallpox epidemic in two towns. Both women become more charitable under the influence of Nazarín, but the change is deeper and more lasting in Beatriz. The three wanderers perform minor tasks for others and receive alms and food in exchange. As time goes on, however, unfounded rumors begin to spread that they are thieves and that Nazarín has illicit relations with one of the two women. It is also rumored that Nazarín and Andara are wanted by authorities in Madrid. The two are arrested, Nazarín is thrown into jail where he is beaten, and finally taken out sick and half-conscious to be delivered to the authorities in Madrid.

Both Nazarín and Beatriz appeared in *Halma* (1895), which follows *Nazarín*. Beatriz aids the condesa de Halma in charitable work and Nazarín is put under Halma's custody by the ecclesiastical authorities, who are puzzled by the contradiction of his saintly serenity and his—to their way of thinking—inexplicable radical conduct. Nazarín performs the role of a wise spiritual counsellor to Halma.

Nazarín tells the wealthy Pedro del Belmonte that love of God begins with love of one's fellow man: "Ignoro si siente usted el amor de Dios; pero sin el del prójimo, aquel grande amor es imposible, pues la planta amorosa tiene sus raíces en nuestro suelo, raíces que son el cariño a nuestros semejantes, y si estas raíces están secas, ¿cómo hemos de esperar flores ni frutos allá arriba?" (v, 1784). Nazarín certainly reveals his love of God through his love of his neighbor. Even though the priest lives from begging, he shares the little food and money that he has with other needy people (v, 1710–1711, 1712).

The love of Nazarín is not sentimental, but objective and knowledgeable; he rejects superstition. When Andara expects him to perform a miracle to cure a baby in Móstoles, he gently reproves her: "La compasión, hija mía, el amor de Cristo y del prójimo no son medicina para el cuerpo" (v, 1712). Finally, the women's insistence that Nazarín can perform miracles elicits a stronger rebuke from the priest. He tells them to believe in science and to put God above science (v, 1714). That Nazarín's love is guided by knowledge is also evident later in his compassionate advice to Beatriz when she shows symptoms of hysteria. He tells her to be convinced that it is an illness of the imagination which must be cured by the imagination (v, 1716).

In the work that Nazarín, along with Beatriz and Andara, does in the two towns ravaged by a smallpox epidemic, he shows the same respect for science as if he were mindful of Christ's injunction to "render therefore to Caesar the things that are Caesar's, and to God the things that are God's." When government doctors with drugs arrive in one of the towns, Nazarín and his companions leave and go to another town to perform the same tasks there until the doctors also arrive in that town (v, 1735-1736).

The greatest trial of Nazarín's love for his fellow man is the abuse which he receives in the jail at the hands of the other prisoners. After having been ridiculed and badly beaten one night, he wakes up the next morning telling them that he forgives them, and would suffer great martyrdom that they might not be lost forever (v, 1756-1757). Nazarín emphasizes that each individual must follow his own conscience in religious matters. "Cada cual con su conciencia, cada cual con su soledad" (v, 1717) is the reply which he gives to Andara when she implores him to let Beatriz accompany him (v, 1717). Nazarín allows both of the women to accompany him, but he teaches them largely by example rather then by precept. He seldom preaches, but speaks quietly with those who want to hear him (v, 1685, 1749).

In his conversation with Pedro del Belmonte, Nazarín advocates the imitation of the life of Christ. He would get rid of the formal trappings of religion. Again indicating the superiority of teaching by example to preaching, he explains his ideas on the type of religion needed by the modern world:

Se necesitan ejemplos, no fraselogia gastada. No basta predicar la doctrina de Cristo, sino darle existencia en la práctica e imitar su vida en lo que es posible a lo humano imitar lo divino para que la Fe acabe de propagarse, en el estado actual de la sociedad, conviene que sus mantenedores renuncien a los artificios que vienen de la Historia, como los torrentes bajan de la montaña, y que patrocinen y practiquen la verdad elemental. (v, 1726)

In addition to his active practice of charity, another important way in which Nazarín imitates Christ is the resignation with which he accepts adversity. On resignation, he says this to Belmonte, bespeaking his conviction that there is a positive force in resignation: "De la resignación absoluta ante el mal no puede menos de salir el bien, como de la mansedumbre sale al cabo la fuerza" (v, 1727). The priest's resignation in the face of mistreatment is tested several times (v, 1711, 1736, 1743). The greatest test of his ability to remain true to the principle of resignation is the abuse he receives in the jail already mentioned above.

From the ideological standpoint, what is important in *Nazarín,* is the movement away from reliance upon authority and theology in religious matters and the movement toward an imitation of the life of Christ. The conscience becomes the ultimate arbiter of the individual's conduct, not authority. Furthermore, the illusion of a dichotomy between love of God and love of man is shattered; love of God becomes unthinkable without love of man.

The spontaneous charity in *Halma* of the condesa de Halma is contrasted with the attitude toward charity of the church official, the priest Manuel Flórez. When Halma wants to reserve a part of a sum of money set aside for the establishment and operation of a charitable institution for distribution among the needy, Flórez objects: "Sí; pero eso es difícil, porque no tendríamos ni para empezar. La caridad debe hacerse con método, apoyándose en el criterio de la Iglesia, y favoreciendo los planes de la misma" (v, 1797). Flórez's equilibrium is eventually so upset that he is unable to bear the comparison of his own perfunctory charity with the effusive humanitarian concern of Halma, and he dies disillusioned because he has been remiss in his vocation as a priest.

Like Nazarín, Halma synthesizes love of God with love of man. A young priest, Remigio Díaz, recruited for service in her institution makes the following observation about the condesa's blending of three types of love: "Yo leo en aquella gran alma el amor de Dios en el grado más ardoroso y puro, el amor de la Naturaleza, el amor del prójimo, y veo en el plan de vida de la señora una síntesis admirable de estos tres amores" (v, 1838). Halma's love of her fellow man and nature is revealed in her provision for a school in her institution, the arrangements for a doctor to visit the sick in the area, and the cultivation of the land around the buildings (v, 1850, 1854). Her aid of José Antonio Urrea has already been discussed.

At the end of the novel, Nazarín advises Halma to give up the idea of practicing charity in an institution modeled after worn-out public and religious institutions since civil and ecclesiastical authorities would soon step in with their rules and deprive her of the freedom to help others as she sees fit (v, 1868). Nazarín tells Halma that she should marry José Antonio and practice charity freely, from the sanctuary of her home (v, 1869–1871).

The Charity Practiced by Orozco

The epistolary novel *La incógnita* (1888–1889) and its companion novel *Realidad* (1889), which is written in dialogue, will be treated as one novel in the analysis of the charity practiced by Tomás Orozco since they both deal with the same events and characters and since *La incógnita* is really incomplete without *Realidad*. The principal theme of these two novels is the nature of reality. External events interpreted one way by Manolo Infante, the composer of virtually all of the letters in *La incógnita,* are seen with greater perspective and in greater depth in *Realidad.* This is possible because the words and thoughts of the characters themselves are all that is presented in *Realidad.* Notwithstanding this fact, reality proves to have many appearances even when one has the illusion of observing it directly, and Orozco, the protagonist of *Realidad,* is much more complicated, as Leopoldo Alas has stated,[13] than he might appear at first glance.

Some of the main external events in the novel center around the charitable acts of Orozco. Aside from quietly aiding a number of poor families, Orozco aids the sister of his friend, Federico Viera, while the latter leads an irregular life, dividing his time between his former mistress la Peri and Orozco's wife Augusta, who is now Federico's lover. Because of Orozco's kindness to his sister and his attempts to help him, Viera becomes increasingly conscience-stricken at having betrayed his friend and finally kills himself. Orozco's wife, Augusta, would like to confess her affair with Federico

71

to her husband, but is unable to do so because of the cold air of self-righteous superiority which he has acquired in his efforts to perfect himself.

There is no doubt that Orozco performs charitable acts; what is difficult to discern is whether or not Galdós considers the charity of his protagonist as completely laudable. Although critics of these two novels have held varying opinions as to the degree of Galdós's approval of Orozco's charity,[14] a close reading of the two novels reveals that the novelist's opinion is not entirely favorable.

Much evidence leading to this conclusion is revealed upon examining the motivation of Orozco. There are two aspects to his motivation: (1) a vague feeling of guilt arises from the fact that the wealth he enjoys is derived from the profits his father and Joaquín Viera, the father of Federico, realized when their insurance company, La Humanitaria, apparently went bankrupt, swallowing thus the savings of hundreds of people and (2) the charity of Orozco becomes progressively an instrument of his own perfection rather than a means of helping others.

In *La incógnita,* Infante writes that Orozco seems visibly affected whenever La Humanitaria is mentioned: "Pero se me figura a mí que su fortuna por la calidad de los materiales que la formaron veinte años ha, pesa bastante sobre su conciencia. Me fundo para creerlo así en la cara que pone cuando le hablan de La Humanitaria" (v, 715–716). The vague guilt which Orozco feels is expressed in his own words: "¡Ay! Esa maldita 'Humanitaria' ha dejado tras sí un restro vergonzoso. Yo no soy responsable; pero disfruto del capital que se amasó con aquel negocio" (v, 808). Thus, in spite of Orozco's ability to absolve himself of guilt from a rational standpoint, it is still evident by the heat of his words that he feels a debt that he cannot discharge.

At least it cannot be discharged directly; it can be discharged through charity, however. It is in this manner that he pays a debt remaining after the liquidation of La Humanitaria, a debt bought at a small percentage of its worth by Joaquín Viera. When Joaquín threatens to sue Orozco for the full amount of the debt, the latter refuses to yield, knowing that the disreputable Viera would prefer a small profit to subjecting the case to the entanglements of Spanish law. Knowing that the debt probably cost Viera less than fifteen percent of its total value, Orozco gives him twenty-five percent and plans to give the remaining seventy-five percent to Clotilde and Federico, Joaquín's neglected offspring. Orozco calls this, fulfilling the spirit of the moral law, "un acto de alta justicia" (v, 854). He is obviously pleased at being able to go beyond the letter of the law in a debt connected with La Humanitaria and dispose of it with such well-directed generosity, since after giving Viera twenty-five percent of the total value, he is under no further obligation.

The second aspect of Orozco's motivation has to do with his increasing use of charity as an instrument of self-perfection. A broad spectrum of opinion is expressed by the other characters as to the merit of Orozco's charity. These attitudes range from the refusal of Cisneros, Orozco's father-in-law, to see any merit in his charity (v, 767) to the unadulterated admiration of it expressed by Federico Viera. Augusta, who is the only one of Orozco's critics with an opportunity to observe his conduct in privacy, tells Infante early in *La incógnita* that she cannot sufficiently praise the goodness of her husband (v, 710-711). At the end of the first *Jornada* in *Realidad,* she is beginning to have doubts about him, however. When Orozco has insomnia and is struggling to perfect his conscience, Augusta, tired of hearing about his delicate scruples thinks to herself: "En ti no hay más que fantasmas, ideas representativas, figuras vestidas de vicios y virtudes, que se mueven con cuerdas. Si eso es la santidad yo no sé si debo desearla" (v, 810). At the end of the second *Jornada,* Augusta confides to Federico that "de algún tiempo a esta parte noto en la bondad de mi marido cierta exaltación de mal agüero, algo así como . . . vamos, que la virtud ha llegado a ser en él una manía, un tic" (v, 828). The third *Jornada* ends with similar doubts on the part of Augusta about the sanity of her husband. When, after he has made the plans to help Clotilde and Federico instead of paying their father the full amount of a debt, Orozco exults over the superior condition of his conscience, Augusta asks herself: "¿Es grandeza de alma en su grado mayor o ebullición intelectual producida por un desquiciamiento del cerebro?"

73

(v, 854). Early in the fifth *Jornada,* Augusta tells Federico that she has been observing Orozco closely and that his aversion to accepting gratitude "no es sino locura" (v, 884). Federico's reaction to Augusta's revelations is to defend Orozco's actions as sublime. He accuses her of not being able to understand Orozco because of her own sin—her adulterous relations with him (v, 743).

Actually neither Augusta nor Federico is capable of seeing Orozco objectively. If Augusta feels too few pangs of conscience as a result of her adultery, Federico is unmercifully subjected to remorse. He is betraying a friend who exhibits unwonted generosity toward him. He would have to be as monstrous as his father if his conscience failed to rebel in such a situation. The truth then, would seem to be relative —dependent upon the personality and circumstances of the individual. But this is not the total picture; the conduct of Orozco himself must be examined.

Orozco exhibits a rare insensitivity to the psychological need of those he has helped to express gratitude. He takes great pains, often unsuccessfully to assure that the good he does is not bruited about. He repeatedly indicates that there is no merit in the good that one does if it is recognized: "Lo que más me enoja es que me aplaudan, como si fuera yo un cómico. Quiero que mis actos sean tan secretos que nadie los penetre: más aun quiero que resulten con apariencias de maldad, para que el mundo los censure y los ridiculice . . . Nada me molesta tanto como la gratitud y las manifestaciones de ella" (v, 1806).

What this statement reveals is callousness on the part of Orozco to the natural need of the recipient of charity to express his gratitude, thus releasing a certain tension which he feels on being indebted to his benefactor. Not only is this revealed, but more importantly what comes to the fore here is that helping others is not so much an end in itself for Orozco as it is a means to his own moral perfection. His aversion to gratitude is based on the assumption that since gratitude is a means of paying him back for what he has done, the beneficiary is, by virtue of his gratitude, morally equal to him; and Orozco wants to surpass everyone else morally. What person really interested in the moral advancement of mankind could actually wish for the world to be full of ingrates, as does Orozco?: "Verdad que hay muchos ingratos, y esto ya es un consuelo" (v, 806). The ambition to be morally superior to others underlies the following statement made by Orozco to Augusta: "Me conviene que continúe este lazo que al mundo nos une, y aparentar que, lejos de haber en mí perfecciones, soy lo mismo que los demás" (v, 807). It is obvious here that Orozco believes that he has already attained a higher moral level than other people.

After the suicide of Federico when Orozco has learned of the liaison between his wife and his friend, his feeling of superiority to ordinary mortals becomes intensified. His cold air of superiority alienates Augusta, making her unable to confess her wrongdoing to him: "Siento en mi alma la expansión religiosa; pero el dogma frío and teórico de este hombre no me entra. Prefiero arrodillarme en el confesioario de cualquier iglesia" (v, 897). When Orozco is convinced that Augusta is not going to confess, he fortifies himself against jealousy with these thoughts:

¿Es decoroso para el espíritu de un hombre afanarse por esto [jealousy]? No: elevar tales menudencias al foro de la conciencia universal es lo mismo que si al ver una hormiga, dos hormigas o cuatro o cien, llevando a rastras un grano de cebada, fuéramos a dar parte a la Guardia Civil y al juez de primera instancia. No: conservemos nuestra calma frente a estas agitaciones microscópicas, para despreciarlas más hondamente. (v, 899)

The coldness with which Orozco treats his wife and his refuge in a world of principles is similar enough to the posture of Maximiliano Rubín, when Fortunata is unfaithful to him, to make the reader suspicious of the healthiness of Orozco's reactions; and the hallucination which the "saint" has at the end of the novel confirms his suspicions (v, 899–901). One of the functions of the hallucinated conversation between Orozco and Federico is to reveal the reason for Federico's suicide, i.e., his inability to quiet his conscience in the face of the generosity of the man whose wife he had taken. It is true that Orozco has a deeper insight into the cause of the suicide of Federico than the other characters in the novels, but it is just as true that he has a hallucination, indicating his precarious mental condition.

There can be little doubt that Orozco's charity does good; what is harmful about it is that in the process of using others as instruments for his own moral elevation, he develops a disdain of them which results in his alienation from them—he is even unable to communicate with his wife. In the final analysis this reveals the massive, but subtle egoism of Orozco, not his charitableness.

Notes

[1] See Leopoldo Alas [Clarín], *Galdós* (1912), p. 34; Julio R. Cejador y Frauca, *Historia de la literatura castellana* (1918), 8: 422; Scatori, passim; L. B. Walton, pp. 66, 228; José A. Balseiro, *Novelistas españoles modernos* (1963), p. 177; Gustavo Correa, *El simbolismo religioso en las novelas de Pérez Galdós* (1962), pp. 23-24; J. Angeles, "Baroja y Galdós: un ensayo de diferenciación," *Revista de literatura,* 23 (1963): 53.

[2] For comments on the ethical nature of Galdós's novels, see Balseiro, p. 167; Agustín Yañez, "Traza de la novela galdosiana," *Cuadernos Americanos,* 11 (1943): 235; Ángel del Río, "Aspectos del pensamiento moral de Galdós," *Cuadernos Americanos,* 13 (1943): 151-152; José Angeles, "¿Galdós precursor del noventa y ocho?" *Hispania,* 46 (1963): 271.

[3] The English philosopher, Bertrand Russell, in *Religion and Science* (1961), speaking of the decay of primitive theological systems makes this comment with which Galdós would undoubtedly have agreed: "But as men grow more reflective there is a tendency to lay less stress on rules and more on states of mind. . . . What they value is a state of mind, out of which, as they hold, right conduct must ensue; rules seem to them external, and insufficiently adaptable to circumstances" (p. 224). Antonio Regalado García, affirming Galdós's recurrence to a religious solution to social problems in *Nazarín, Halma,* and *Misericordia* which, in his view, is traditional, overlooks in his *Benito Pérez Galdós y la novela histórica española* (1966) Galdós's modern emphasis on emotional states as opposed to the stress laid on rules by traditional religion (see pp. 208-209).

[4] Hilario Sáenz, in his "Vision galdosiana de la religiosidad de los españoles," *Hispania,* 20 (1937): 237, has pointed out that the *santurronas* are seldom really charitable.

[5] Susanne Langer, in *Philosophy in a New Key: A Study in the Symbolism of Reason, Rite, and Art* (1956), describes a nondiscursive form as a symbol of an aspect of reality too newly apprehended to be described in conventional terms. Discursive language is conventional language such as is used by ordinary historians or textbook writers. Examples of nondiscursive forms are poems, novels, paintings, symphonies, etc. (see Ch. IV, "Discursive and Presentational Forms," pp. 63-83.)

[6] Miguel de Unamuno, *Del sentimiento trágico de la vida* (1961), p. 237.

[7]For comments by critics on the importance given by Galdós to the conscience, see César Barja, *Libros y autores modernos* (1933), p. 363; Angel del Río, "Aspectos del pensamiento moral de Galdós," *Cuadernos Americanos*, 12 (1943): 152; Eoff, *The Novels of Pérez Galdós: The Concept of Life as Dynamic Process* (1954), pp. 115–116.

[8]*Hispanic Studies in Honor of Nicholson B. Adams* (1966), p. 155.

[9]Balseiro, p. 168.

[10]*Human Society in Ethics and Politics* (1955), pp. 19–21.

[11]For further discussion of this theme in *Gloria,* see Alas, pp. 39–61; Joaquín Casalduero, *Vida y obra de Galdós* (1961), pp. 59–61; H. C. Borrowitz, *Pérez Galdós: The Spanish Liberal Crusader* (1948), pp. 71–72; Correa, pp. 49–62.

[12]v, 1178, 1180. Without specifically mentioning the doctrine of hell, Galdós in 1865 in his "Crónica de Madrid," dismisses the idea of the existence of the devil as superstition (vi, 1530).

[13]Leopoldo Alas (Clarín), "Review of *Realidad, novela en cinco jornadas,*" by Benito Pérez Galdós, *La España Moderna,* 13: (1890), 223.

[14]See, for example Leopoldo Alas, *Galdós,* pp. 199–200, 229; Casalduero, pp. 100–102; R. Kirsner, "Galdós Attitude Toward Spain as seen in the Characters of *Fortunata y Jacinta,*" *PMLA,* 66 (1951): 129; Eoff, *The Novels of Pérez Galdós,* pp. 143–144; Monroe Z. Hafter, "Ironic Reprise in Galdós' Novels," *PMLA,* 76 (1961): 238–239.

IV   Misericordia

INASMUCH AS Misericordia (1897) represents Galdós's most affirmative and synthetic dramatization of the practice of charity, the novel deserves separate treatment. Through the conduct of a lowly servant, Benigna (Benina), Galdós dramatizes the view that ultimately human relationships are spiritual. In her dealings with the other characters of the novel, Benina gives precedence to charity over all other considerations in interpersonal relationships. The traditional molds of society for determining the nature of the relationship between one individual and another are considered by Benina to be of little importance. Differences in individuals of class, creed, race, profession, and nationality melt away before the warmth of charity.[1] Social decorum is of secondary importance—a luxury for the poor people with whom Benina deals. Benina's charity is effusive, but not sentimental; she leaves no ends untied to provide for those who depend upon her, yet she will put up with no nonsense from those who would refuse her aid out of pride or those who would squander the small sums which she has so diligently gotten together. At the end of the novel, Benina has a sense of fulfillment and tranquility of conscience unknown to those who have had some criterion other than charity as the basis of their human relationships.

In the opening pages of *Misericordia*, Galdós reveals the world in which Benina must live. The initial scene with the beggars around the doors of the Church of San Sebastián is one of the most graphic descriptions of such a group in Spanish literature. Aside from Galdós's purpose of providing the background for Benina's activity, he also obviously relishes the *costumbrista* aspect of the description.

Speaking of how the beggars place themselves at the doors of the church, Galdós insinuates that one of their functions is to relieve the conscience of the malefactor by accepting his alms: "Mucho más numerosa y formidable que por el Sur es por el Norte la cuadrilla de miseria que acecha el paso de la caridad, al modo de guardia de alcabaleros que cobra humanamente el portazgo en la frontera de lo divino o la contribución impuesta a las conciencias impuras, que van a donde lavan" (v, 1877).

Galdós then goes on to remark on the professionalism of these beggars, revealing the hierarchy that exists among them in the distribution of collective alms: "En las limosnas colectivas y en los repartos de bonos, llevaban preferencia las *antiguas;* y cuando algún parroquiano daba una cantidad cualquiera para que fuese distribuída entre todos, la antigüedad reclamaba derecho a la repartición, apropiándose la cifra mayor si la cantidad no era fácilmente divisible en partes iguales" (v, 1181).[2]

It is clear later that Galdós wishes to stress the magnitude of the problem of poverty in Spain, when the charitable priest don Romualdo makes this hyperbolic statement upon learning that doña Paca has been supported by Benina's begging: "Podríamos creer—añadió—que es nuestro país inmensa gusanera de pobres, y que debemos hacer de la nación un asilo sin fin, donde quepamos todos, desde el primero al último. Al paso que vamos, pronto seremos el más grande hospicio de Europa" (v, 1968).

Although Benina is the servant of doña Francisco Juárez (doña Paca), her position is of little real importance in her relationship with her mistress and the latter's children, Obdulia and Antoñito. Besides being a servant she occupies the position of an old friend. Doña Paca is over sixty years old and ailing; thus it is necessary for Benina to support her if she is to have her daily needs met. Although Benina must beg to do this, she carefully conceals this fact from the snobbish doña Paca by inventing the fiction that don Romualdo, a charitable priest, employs her during the day (v, 1891). Doña Paca's irresponsible childishness requires that Benina take full responsibility for her support, yet her mistress's pride makes it necessary to deceive her about the origin and the amount of money that she has (v, 1895). After doña Paca's financial ruin Benina, through her knowledge of prices, economized when her mistress sent her to the market. Her purpose was to secretly set aside a sum of money for future use. The novelist indicates that she never loses this habit of hiding money from her mistress (v, 1899). Benina, completely oblivious of conventional social decorum, also lies to her mistress. When she has to employ two *duros,* which don Carlos Moreno Trujillo gives her, to help others who depend upon her, Benina assuages the anger of her mistress by telling her that don Carlos only gave them a black book for keeping account of their income and expenses (v, 1927–1928).

While the methods of Benina may be somewhat Machiavellian on a small scale, her purpose is charitable and she harms no one by her violations of social mores.[3] Benina's cutting of social corners is for the benefit of others, as the novelist indicates here:

> Con esfuerzos sobrehumanos, empleando la actividad corpórea, la atención intensa y la inteligente travesura, *Benina* le [a doña Paca] daba de comer lo mejor posible, a veces muy bien, con delicadezas refinadas. Un profundo sentimiento de caridad la movía, y además el ardiente cariño que a la señora profesaba, como para compensarla, a su manera, de tantas desdichas y amarguras. Conformábase ella con chupar algunos huesos y catar desperdicios siempre y cuando doña Paca quedase satisfecha. Pero no por caritativa y cariñosa perdía sus mañas instintivas; siempre ocultaba a su señora una parte del dinero, trabajosamente reunido, y la guardaba para formar nuevo fondo y capital nuevo. (v, 1899)[4]

Furthermore, the loving care Benina has given to doña Paca's two children in the past and the solicitous care she gives to Obdulia when her husband neglects her involve a considerable expenditure of time and energy.[5]

The principal aspect of Benina's relationship with Frasquito Ponte, the aging fop who is Obdulia's friend, is her charitableness toward him. Knowing that he is so poor that he is forced to sleep in a cheap hotel, Benina invites him to eat with her and Obdulia one day when she finds him visiting in Obdulia's house. Mindful that Ponte has the pride of one who has not always been poor, Benina asks him to honor them by sharing a meal with them (v, 1916–1917, 1922). When Ponte leaves, Benina hastens after him to give him a *peseta* to pay for sleeping quarters. She tells him not to be finicky, that she knows that he is as poor as she is. Ponte first turns pale, then blushes at this frontal attack on his sense of decorum, but the charity of Benina is armed with the logic of the truth and he keeps the coin which his benefactress thrusts into his hand, calling her an angel while his eyes fill with tears of irritation, admiration, and gratitude (v, 1925–1926). Later, when Benina learns that Ponte is sick and has no one to care for him, she brings him to doña Paca's house, gives him her own bed, and cares for him (v, 1935–1936). Godlike in her sense of responsibility, Benina spares no effort in taking care of Ponte, protecting him from the delirious conversation of Obdulia by persuading her not to visit him (v, 1938), and advising his employers of the reason for his absence: "Como a todo atendía Nina, y ninguna necesidad de las personas sometidas a su cuidado se le olvidaba, creyó conveniente avisar a las señoras de la Constanilla de San Andres, que de seguro habrían extrañado la ausencia de su dependiente" (IV, 1951).

Except for the Moroccan, Almudena, Ponte is the only one of Benina's beneficiaries who reveals unequivocal gratitude for having received help from her. Such is his concern for her that he organizes a group to go to have her released from El Pardo, where she has been detained for begging on a proscribed street (v, 1974–1975, 1979–1980). There is poetic justice in the radical transformation that Benina undergoes in the eyes of Ponte when, after having received a blow on the head as a result of a fall from his horse, he comes into doña Paca's house raving that he has not made amorous overtures to Benina as he has been accused of doing: "Me acusan de un infame delito: de haber puesto mis ojos en un ángel, de blancas alas célicas, de pureza inmaculada: si *Nina* fuese criatura mortal, no la habría respetado, porque soy hombre . . . la Nina no es de este mundo . . . , La *Nina* pertenece al cielo . . ." (v, 1989).[6] A few moments later, Ponte dies of a sudden attack related to his fall from the horse.

That Benina's charity knows no bounds is evident in her

compassion for Petra, the alcoholic who shares living quarters with Almudena. When the latter becomes impatient with the drunkenness of Petra, Benina, full of understanding, advises him not to beat her for getting drunk again: "y a esta pobre desgraciada, cuando despierte, no la pegues, hijo, ¡pobrecita! Cada uno, por el aquel de no sufrir, se emborracha con lo que puede: ésta con el aguardentazo, otros con otra cosa" (v, 1889).

On one occasion when Benina is surrounded by needy people in a poor neighborhood, they confuse her because of her charitable acts with the aristocratic doña Guillermina Pacheco who years before had distributed money and goods among the poor. The narrator asks rhetorically,

> ¿Cómo podía ser confundida con ella, con la infeliz Benina? A cien leguas se conocía en esta a una mujer del pueblo, criada de servir. Si por su traje pobrísimo, lleno de remiendos y zurcidos; por sus alpargatas rotas, no comprendían ellos la diferencia entre una cocinera jubilada y una señora nacida de marqueses, pues bien pudiera ésta vestirse de máscara, en otras cosas no cabía engaño ni equivocación: por ejemplo, en el habla. (v, 1956)

The implication is that Benina and doña Guillermina are equals in the important trait of charitableness. Class lines are momentarily blurred so that Benina's external conditions are seen as unimportant when compared with the superior condition of her soul. The superiority of Benina's spontaneous practice of charity stands in sharp contrast to the calculated giving of don Carlos Moreno Trujillo, the moderately wealthy husband of doña Paca's now defunct sister. He keeps, by his own admission, a daily, monthly, and yearly account of the alms that he gives (v, 1905–1906). Early in *Misericordia* he enters the church of San Sebastián giving alms in a measured fashion to the beggars who in turn distribute the money among themselves according to their rank in the hierarchy of their profession. One of the beggars, mindful of don Carlos's regularity exclaims: "don Carlos sabe cumplir y paga lo que debe" (v, 1880). Doña Paca explains that don Carlos has made his wealth through smuggling and by bribing customs officials; according to her, he expects to bribe his way into heaven: "Porque ése no se acerca a los pobres sino con su cuenta y razón. Cree que repartiendo limosnas de ochavo y proporcionándose por poco precio las oraciones de los humildes podrá engañar al de arriba y estafar la gloria eterna, o colarse en el cielo de contrabando, haciéndose pasar por lo que no es" (v, 1903).

The unkindness of the miserly don Carlos and his late wife to doña Paca, when she was ruined financially, should not lead the reader to discount her opinion of the miser as unreliable.[7] Proof of his miserly calculation is revealed in an interview that he has with Benina, doña Paca's maid and friend. Expecting to receive a considerable gift of money, Benina receives first a lecture on the necessity of being orderly in financial matters. Then, the miser declares that the best gift that he can give doña Paca is a black book in which she can keep account of her income and expenses. After receiving Benina's assurance that she will pray for him and his wife, Don Carlos takes out twelve duros, passes them from one hand to the other, and indicates that he will dole them out to her at the rate of two a month. At the end of six months, he will check the accounts doña Paca has kept and will decide then whether the alms should be increased or decreased (v, 1905–1907). Benina's first reaction to the hypocritical farce of don Carlos is anger; then she makes an attempt to see him in perspective: "no puede hacer más de lo que le manda su natural. Válgate Dios: si cosas muy raras cría Nuestro Señor en el aquel de persona. No acaba una de ver verdades que parecen mentiras. . . . En fin, otros son peores que este don Carlos, que al cabo da algo, aunque sea por cuenta y apuntación.... Peores los hay, y tan peores . . . que ni apuntan ni dan" (v, 1907).

Benina's approach to helping others is also preferable to that of the governmental institutions established for the benefit of the poor. The manner in which Benina is taken to San Bernardino, a house of correction for beggars, when she is caught begging in a prohibited area, reveals the callousness of the municipal authorities with regard to the dignity and needs of the poor. Benina is approached by a policeman, who shoves her rudely and orders her to move on without informing her as to where he is taking her. When she does learn where he is taking her, she feels offended for being treated as if she were a common criminal (v, 1961). The municipal authorities are entirely oblivious of the inconvenience caused Benina by her arrest. Her principal concern is that those who depend upon her, doña Paca and Ponte, will suffer hunger that night (v, 1961-1962). Thus, a poor beggar is portrayed as having a greater sense of responsibility than an institution ostensibly set up for the welfare of the poor.

The relationship of Benina with the blind Moroccan beggar, Almudena, who confesses to be of the Jewish religion, reveals that human relationships only attain their deepest meaning when accidents of social position, nationality, and religion are overlooked and love is allowed to serve as the common denominator in relationships between individuals. Almudena and Benina are seen as friends in the beginning of the novel (v, 1889-1907)—Almudena gives Benina some money which she needs, and they discuss social injustice and religion (v, 1908-1909). Later, Benina must gently explain to Almudena that her help involves nothing more than charity, when the impulsive beggar tells her that he is in love with her and proposes marriage (v, 1953-1954). While Benina is engaged in charitable activities for others, she loses track of Almudena temporarily. She then traces him to a rough section of Madrid and brings him food which he scarcely notices because of his protestations of love (v, 1953-1954).

The real proof of Benina's equalitarian charity is when, after their release from El Pardo, she brings Almudena, who has a repugnant skin disease, to doña Paca's house to care for him there. The conversation between servant and mistress reveals their spiritual differences: "A casa la traía porque está enfermo, y no le voy a dejar en medio de la calle—replicó *Benina* con firme acento" (v, 1982). Doña Paca's reply indicates a greater concern for social decorum than for human suffering: "Ya sé que eres buena, y que a veces tu bondad te ciega y no miras por el decoro" (v, 1982). Benina makes no distinction between Almudena and Ponte:

84

A casa le traía, si señora, como traje a Frasquito Ponte, por caridad. . . . Si hubo misericordia con el otro, ¿por qué no ha de haberla con éste? ¿O es que la caridad es una para el caballero de levita y otra para el pobre desnudo? yo no lo entiendo así, yo no distingo. . . . Por eso le traía; si a él no le admite, será lo mismo si a mí no me admitiera. (v, 1982)

This occurs after the arrival of don Romualdo with the news of an inheritance for doña Paca, her children, and Ponte. Doña Paca's refusal to allow Benina to stay with her any longer is Juliana's decision. As soon as the news of the doña Paca's inheritance arrives, her energetic and domineering daughter-in-law Juliana appears on the scene to demonstrate her ambition to handle the large sums of money which promise to be available. It is Juliana who is in charge of the affairs of the family when Benina is released and returns home with the blind and sick Moor, Almudena. Juliana, usurping the authority of the passive doña Paca, has Benina thrown out of the house permanently, despite her past support of her mother-in-law, and in spite of her loving care of doña Paca's two children from the earliest years of their childhood. Juliana excuses her action by advising doña Paca that she has a cousin who will make a better servant.

Juliana is not to perform such a monstrous act with impunity, however; within the month she begins to pay tribute to her conscience: "Comenzó el mal de Juliana por insomnios rebeldes: se levantaba todas las mañanas sin haber pegado los ojos; a los pocos días del insomnio empezó a perder el apetito, y por fin, al no dormir se agregaron sobresaltos y angustiosos temores por las noches, y de día una melancolía negra, pesada, funebre" (v, 1991). Her illness finally crystallizes into the delusion that her twins are sick (v, 1991).

She reveals the origin of her psychological disturbance when she seeks out Benina using as a pretext the former servant's failure to come by the house each day for two reales and the leftovers which had been promised her. She brings the accumulated reales with her, exclaiming "me pesan en la conciencia" (v, 1991). Juliana tells Benina of the illness she suffers and her fear that her twins are dying, but she leaves hastily before Benina can combat this delusion effectively. The next morning she returns in a state of agitation, fearful for the lives of her children. She is obsessed with the idea that only Benina can cure her of this fixed idea by affirming that the children are well. Benina complies and dismisses Juliana with a command that reveals her insight into the more or less subconscious feeling of guilt at the root of the delusion: "No llores . . . , y ahora vete a tu casa, y no vuelvas a pecar" (v, 1992).

The superiority of Benina's approach to human relations as contrasted with other approaches presented in the novel is manifest when the story ends. When don Romualdo appears and insists that he is not the charitable don Romualdo whom Benina has invented, doña Paca remains unconvinced, thinking that he is modest about the charity which he practices: "Es propio de las grandes almas caritativas esconderse, negar su propia personalidad, para de este modo huir del agradecimiento y de la publicidad de sus virtudes . . . (v, 1967). Yet when it becomes apparent moments later that the description which she has just made applies more logically to Benina she is scandalized rather than grateful that her maid has supported her by begging.[8] Social prejudice blinds her to the true virtue of Benina's conduct. Doña Paca, however, is not happy after receiving her inheritance; she lives fearfully under the domination of the energetic Juliana (v, 1978-1990). Her sadness arouses compassion in Benina: "¡Pobre señora mía!—dijo al ciego en cuanto se reunía con él—. La quiero como hermana, porque juntas hemos pasado muchas penas. Yo era todo para ella, y ella todo para mí. ¡Me perdonaba mis faltas y yo le perdonaba las suyas . . . ! Que triste va, quizá pensando en lo mal que se ha portado con la *Nina*" (v, 1988).

Benina, on the other hand, in spite of suffering from the ingratitude of doña Paca and her family, at the end of the novel, has a sense of fulfillment. The novelist describes her feelings this way:

Las adversidades se estrellaban ya en el corazón de *Benina* como las vagas olas en el robusto cantil. Rompíanse con estruendo, se quebraban, se deshacían en blancas espumas y nada más. . . . Su conciencia le dió inefables consuelos: miró la vida desde la altura en que su desprecio de la humana vanidad le ponía; vió en ridícula pequeñez a los seres que la rodeaban, y su

espíritu se hizo fuerte y grande. Había alcanzado glorioso tri-
unfo; sentíase victoriosa. después de haber perdido la batalla
en el terreno material. (v, 1986) [9]

The victory of Benina has none of the ambiguity of Orozco's
self-consciously attained virtue; her actions establish un-
equivocally the priority of charity in human relationships.[10]

Notes

[1] The blurring of class distinctions and the equalitarian tendency of
Benina's conduct has been pointed out by Angel del Río, *Estudios galdosianos* (1953), pp. 25, 26.

[2] For further descriptions of the beggars of San Sebastián, see v, 1882–
1886, 1929.

[3] Benina engaged in petty theft in doña Paca's house in the past (v,
1894). Once when doña Paca was in a bad mood she attempted to humili-
ate Benina by reminding her of this (v, 1945).

[4] For other instances in which Benina sacrifices herself for doña Paca,
see v, 1894–1895, 1902, 1927–1928, 1981–1982.

[5] For examples, see v, 1894, 1896, 1900, 1901, 1907, 1916, 1959.

[6] For a discussion of Benina's angelic condition, see Gustavo Correa,
El simbolismo religioso en las novelas de Pérez Galdós (1962), pp. 206–207.

[7] The Moreno Trujillos took advantage of doña Paca's financial diffi-
culties by buying up the furniture that she was forced to sell for almost
nothing. They refused to offer her a loan, yet hypocritically presented
themselves as her saviors when her furniture was on the verge of being
confiscated (v, 1904).

[8] v, 1967–1968. Though the cases differ in many ways, doña Paca's
reaction of shame to the knowledge that she has been supported by a
beggar is similar to Pip's feelings in Dickens's *Great Expectations* when he
learns that he has been made a gentleman through the support of the con-
vict Magwitch. As in the case of doña Paca, Pip's shabby treatment of
Magwitch is based on a perversion of values. Unlike doña Paca, Pip finally
shows compassion toward Magwitch.

[9] In *El audaz* (1871) Galdós dramatizes how a man is destroyed through
his violent rebellion against social injustice. In *Misericordia,* don Benito
demonstrates how even the most lowly of persons can attain fulfillment
through love in spite of social injustice. Benina is a positive alternative to
Martín Muriel's destructive reaction to social inequities.

[10] Love is also the principal theme of *El abuelo.* At the end of the novel
Albrit has learned that love is more important than blood ties (vi, 111–112).

V Charity as a Factor in Characterization, Plot, and Setting

Characterization and Tone

While situations involving charity play a role in adding to the complexity of characterization in Galdós's *Novelas de la primera época* as well as in the *Novelas españolas contemporáneas,* there is a discernible qualitative difference in this respect in the two periods. The more gradual and more extensive accumulation of details about characters in the second group of novels tends to make their characters more convincing. Apparently contradictory traits such as charitableness and cruelty are seen in the perspective of a more complex motivation. Consequently, many traits are blended into a single personality more smoothly in the *Novelas españolas contemporáneas* than in the first group of novels, where characters tend to embody abstractions; traits which do not contribute to strengthening the abstractions are often poorly integrated into the characterization because of insufficient motivation.

With regard to characters who are foils in the trait of charitableness there is no discernible difference between the earlier novels and the later ones, unless it be a greater permeability of one of the foils in the later novels, that is, in the ability of one of the foils to influence the other in the trait of charitableness.

With respect to the role which charity plays in the development of characters, the development of a character toward charitableness is more frequently observed in the *Novelas españolas contemporáneas.*

One of Galdós's critics has paid the following tribute to the Spanish novelist's ability to create complex characters: "Galdós hace responsable de sus errores y flaquezas—hasta donde pueden serlo como individuos—a los que conviven en su historia. No los divide como aquellos autores, en dos bandos: angelicales y demoníacos. Entre los perversos y los débiles hallaremos rasgos y admiraremos gestos de bondad y corrección, sin desfigurarse por ello esencialmente."[1]

It is obvious that the addition of any trait to the other attributes of a given character increases the complexity of that character. Therefore, any charitable act by any character in Galdós's novels could be looked upon as increasing the complexity of that character. For this reason, a narrower, but more meaningful criterion must be sought to reveal how Galdós uses the trait of charitableness to make his characters more complex, or to give them a greater "roundness," to use E. M. Forster's term.[2] The cases considered here, then, are those in which the desire for the effect of "roundness" of characterization is one of the principal reasons, or the sole reason, for attributing the trait of charitableness to a character, whether this be done by the author, other characters, or through the acts, words, or thoughts of the characters themselves.

The irascible and unpredictable priest, Pedro Polo, who appears in *El doctor Centeno* as the scourge of the children he purports to teach, and in *Tormento* as the scourge of Amparo Sánchez Emperador, whom he had seduced in bygone years and now wishes to make his lover again, is also shown to have a charitable side to his personality. Don Florencio Morales, a friend of Alejandro Miquis, says to him of Polo: "Lleva el corazón en la mano, y todo cuanto tiene es para los necesitados" (IV, 1305). It is also revealed later in the novel that Polo takes care of his mother and sister: "Aunque la mayor de las satisfacciones de don Pedro Polo era el bienestar de su madre y hermana, a quienes amaba tiernamente" (IV, 1313). And of course he takes the orphaned Felipe Centeno as his servant and admits him to his school (IV, 1317, 1318), an act which reveals good intentions but which is by no means an unalloyed blessing.

In contrast with this charitableness, Polo, the teacher, has an educational philosophy represented by this principle: "'Siembra coscorrones y recogerás sabios'" (IV, 1312). The author indicates that Polo's cruelty as a teacher is based on conviction: "Es forzoso repetir que la crueldad de don Pedro era convicción, y su barbarie fruto áspero, pero madurísimo, de la conciencia. No era un maestro severo, sino un honrado vándalo. Entraba a saco los entendimientos, y arrasaba cuanto se le ponía adelante" (IV, 1315).[3]

In *Tormento,* Polo is embarrassed on being reminded that he had paid for the funeral of Amparo and Refugio's father and had sold some of his clothes to provide food for them (IV, 1500–1501).

Later, when the priest perversely pursues Amparo with the object of making love to her, he is also shown taking care of his aged servant Celedonia instead of sending her to a hospital. Polo explains his care to Amparo: "¡Pobre mujer!—dijo Polo—. No he querido mandarla al hospital. ¿Quién ha de cuidar de ella si yo no la cuido?" (IV, 1535).[4]

A very minor character in *El doctor Centeno* is given a certain "roundness" through the attribute of charitableness. When Alejandro brings Centeno to the boardinghouse in which he stays, the owner of the house, doña Virginia, at first, scolds Alejandro for bringing another sick person off the street for her to feed and lodge, then she relents, letting the boy stay and making jokes about him (IV, 1309–1310).

The aging don Juan Lopez Garrido (don Lope) in *Tristana* (1892) who seduced his young ward Tristana Reluz after her parents died has ambivalent feelings toward her when she becomes enamored of a young man. He struggles between his possessive desire to retain her as a lover and the demands of his conscience to consider her as a daughter. When Tristana's leg is amputated, she writes to her suitor that don Lope has begun to call her his daughter and supply her with books, belatedly regretting his neglect of her education (V, 1584). The novelist also indicates that don Lope is visibly affected by Tristana's suffering: "La quería con entrañable afecto y se acongojaba de verla enferma y con pocas esperanzas de pronto remedio" (V, 1587). Later, his compassion is mixed with a possessive love again, when he exclaims that he is willing to spend the rest of his fortune to cure Tristana (V, 1593–1594). Don Lope marries Tristana finally, after her suitor loses interest in her. But the main point here is the increased complexity of don Lope's characterization, arising from the blending of compassion with less disinterested traits which serve as the basis of his relationship with Tristana.

The charitable attitude of Pepe Rey in *Doña Perfecta* (1876) toward the three Troya sisters, who eke out a meager living in Orbajosa by sewing, contrasts with the ostracism of these young ladies by the leading citizens of the town. Their bad reputation stems in part from their spreading gossip and dropping orange peelings from their balcony on pedestrians. Pepe is moved to compassion when he sees the poverty in which they live: "El aspecto de la miseria, que con horribles esfuerzos pugnaba por no serlo, afligió al joven" (IV, 444). Shortly afterward, the narrator goes on expressing Pepe's feelings toward the sisters: "Pepe Rey sentía hacia ellas una lástima profunda. Observó sus miserables vestidos, compuestos, arreglados y remendados de mil modos para que pareciesen nuevos; observó sus zapatos rotos, y otra vez se llevó la mano al bolsillo" (IV, 445). Before leaving, Pepe gives the Troyas some money, though his manner of doing this is not made explicit (IV, 448).

That evening at dinner, Pepe is attacked by both his aunt, doña Perfecta, and the priest, don Inocencio, for his visit with the Troyas. Doña Perfecta, accuses him, as if his generosity were a crime, of having given money to the sisters (IV, 448). And don Inocencio, in an ironic tone, insinuates that Pepe was momentarily seduced by the charm of the sisters into being a "cómplice de sus desvergonzados y criminales insultos a la vecindad" (IV, 448).[5]

The compassion with which don Francisco Cucúrbitas in *Miau* treats the unemployed former bureaucrat don Ramón Villaamil is in sharp contrast with the abuse the afflicted man receives at the hands of his other acquaintances, including his son-in-law Víctor Cadalso.

Don Ramón considers Cucúrbitas, who has had unfortunate experiences similar to his, as the only one of his bureaucratic acquaintances who is capable of compassion for him in his jobless plight; he indicates this to his wife: "Es la única persona verdaderamente cristiana entre todos mis amigos, un caballero, un hombre de bien, que se hace cargo de las necesidades . . . ¡Qué diferencia de otros!" Don Ramón goes on to describe to his wife how one of his former subordinates, Rubín, had insulted him by sending him a half *duro* when he had asked for a loan (v, 554).

Don Ramón receives financial aid from Cucúrbitas four or five times until his friend must tell him that he can no longer spare the money to help him (v, 555, 557–558).

Contrasted with the good will of Cucúrbitas is the malevolence of the crippled Salvador Guillén who, on government time, draws a caricature of Villaamil, passes it around in the office where he works, and belittles the unemployed man's plan for tax reform (v, 617). On one occasion when he enters the office in which Guillén works, Villaamil observes the mirth of the bureaucrats and rightly suspects that they have been ridiculing him. The diversion had been stimulated by a series of Guillén's caricatures, describing the life of Villaamil (v, 653). The infuriated don Ramón lambasts Guillén for being "el autor de esa porquería," while the crippled bureaucrat cringes, attempting to shift the blame to other shoulders (v, 654).

The bureaucrat who does the greatest harm to Villaamil, however, is his son-in-law Víctor. Víctor hypocritically tells Villaamil's wife that he has looked after his father-in-law's interest before his own in looking for a job (v, 645). Nevertheless, don Ramón learns later from Cucúrbitas that it was precisely Víctor who had sabotaged his efforts to get a job by passing the word around among government officials that his father-in-law was incapable of handling any job for reasons of insanity (v, 650).

Charitableness is often a static trait in the characterization of many of Galdós's characters, that is, the individual's characterization with regard to charitableness is not a developing one. In other cases, where an individual is depicted as growing in charitableness or vice versa, the growth is seen as stimulated by certain psychological, social, or religious and ethical forces upon which the author wishes to focus.

In *La desheredada* charity plays a role in the development of the characterization of the protagonist Isidora Rufete while its ideological importance is secondary. Isidora's reaction to the good will and friendship demonstrated toward her, the sound advice offered her, and the concrete financial aid which she receives from other characters in the novel serves to define her personality. The charitable treatment which she receives at the hands of other characters in the novel serves the function of compensating for her unfavorable environmental conditions. It reveals, moreover, that her eventual lapse into prostitution is in large part an outcome of her own making, not an inevitable result of environmental or hereditary determinism.

Although Eoff has interpreted *Misericordia* as primarily a study of Benina's growth in charitableness, an examination of this novel, has disclosed that its principal significance lies in its emphasis on the supremacy of charity in human relations, rather than on character development.[6]

The objectivity of Galdós's novels led one of his contemporaries to criticize him for his failure to become emotionally involved with his characters.[7] This critic apparently expected to find indications of the novelist's emotional identification with his characters. This is not to imply that Galdós is completely objective in his novels. Galdós developed subtle techniques for implying his attitudes toward what happens in his novels. It may be inferred, from his ability to create "round" characters, that rarely may a given character in a novel be considered as consistently representing his viewpoint. Some characters come much closer to doing this than others, of course, but in order to discern the various shades of the implied attitude of the novelist, a careful examination of the characters, as well as the author's commentary, must be made. In Galdós's novels the tone is a resultant of numerous vectors.

One of the ways that Galdós indicates his attitude toward a character is through attributing to that character the trait of charitableness or uncharitableness. Characters in whose lives charity is a central value are usually closer to being representative of the viewpoint of the novelist than those who are characterized as conspicuously devoid of this trait. This does not mean, however, that Galdós gives a blanket approval to the actions of the characters who are charitable and that he disapproves of all the acts performed by uncharitable characters. Charitable characters may have defects and uncharitable ones, virtues. Moreover, Galdós sometimes attributes charitable acts to a character, the pattern of whose life is negative on the whole, in order to elicit interest and sympathy from the reader on the character's behalf. This is usually the case when there is a tragic element in a character's development. Underlying the attribution of charitableness to a character to aid in establishing the tone of the novel is Galdós's assumption that charitableness is a universally admired trait; thus he can rely on its presence in the actions of a character to elicit a certain amount of sympathy toward that character, while the conspicuous absence of charitableness in a character would naturally evoke the opposite response of repugnance in the reader.

Charity which functions in Galdós's novels is more refined in the *Novelas españolas contemporáneas* than in the earlier *Novelas de la primera época* for the same reason that the novelist's characterization in general is superior in the former group of novels. The characters in the *Novelas de la primera época* tend to embody abstractions, and the reader has little doubt as to where the sympathies of the novelist lie.

The novelist awakens the sympathy of the reader for Gloria Lantigua early in the novel *Gloria* by describing her care for her two young brothers until their death:

Ella misma, después de cuidarlos en su enfermedad con extremado celo, les había cerrado los ojos, les había vestido y les había puesto flores en las sienes y en las manos. . . . Las dos inocentes cariaturas ocuparon siempre lugar muy grande en el corazón de su hermana, y ésta no pasaba sin derramar lágrimas por el rústico cementerio de la villa, donde aquéllos habían dejado su mortal vestidura. (IV, 515)

While Gloria performs other charitable acts, these acts have other functions in addition to evoking a response of sympathy for the protagonist; this is the only discernible function in the description of her care for her brothers.

Galdós has at least two purposes in having León Roch both praise and criticize charitableness of Pepa Fúcar in *La familia de León Roch.* The first is to make her attractive to the reader when León says this: "Haces limosna, amparas a los desvalidos, porque tienes un corazon excelente" (IV, 773). The second reason is to reveal the undisciplined, impulsive side of Pepa's personality which makes it possible for her to commit the error of marrying the ne'er-do-well Federico Cimarra. This side of her nature is revealed in León's criticism of the impulsiveness with which she gives a woman who wishes to celebrate a novena two thousand *reales,* while the widow of a bricklayer who was killed while building the Fúcar mansion receives only a *duro* from her (IV, 773).

In this same novel, the author lets the reader know rather directly what attitude he should take toward León's father-in-law, the marqués de Tellería. The marqués is described as possessing an exterior refinement which belies his total lack of benevolence: "Su vestir correctísimo y elegante, sus ademanes desembarazados, su cortesía refinada y desa-brida, que encubría una falta absoluta de benevolencia, de caridad, de ingenio, adornaban su persona, brillando como la encuadernación de un libro sin ideas" (IV, 982–983).

In *Fortunata y Jacinta* the novelist engages the reader's sympathy for Jacinta before she marries Juanito Santa Cruz. He uses these words and phrases in describing her: "Cariñosa," "corazón amante," and "Pagaba siempre con creces el cariño que se le tenía" (V, 46–47).[8] Jacinta's charitableness is only one way the novelist obtains the reader's benevolence for Jacinta, who is later frustrated by her inability to have children and the infidelity of her husband. The novelist's ap-proval of Jacinta's basic style of life is made evident through his portrayal of Fortunata, the rival for Jacinta's husband's affections. Fortunata develops a greater generosity as a re-sult of her admiration and imitation of Jacinta's style of life.

In this same novel, when Juan Pablo is affectionate with his brother Maxi's future bride, Fortunata, the author promptly short-circuits any temptation the reader may have to inter-pret this behavior as symptomatic of the older brother's gen-eral kindness: "Con gran sorpresa de la novia, Juan Pablo estuvo afectuoso con ella. Creeríase que intentaba hacer rabiar a su tía (doña Lupe) concediendo su benevolencia a la persona de quien aquélla había dicho tantas perrerías" (V, 262–263).

Much later, when Maxi is showing signs of mental de-rangement, Juan Pablo suddenly takes great interest in his brother's mental health, and suggests that he be subjected to

Scottish showers. The reader is not long deluded by Juan Pablos's interest in Maxi's illness, however, for the author informs him that this concern is a lubricant to facilitate the opening of doña Lupe's purse. What he wants is to gain the good will of his aunt so that she will lend him a sum of money (v, 478–479).

Galdós wins the sympathy of the reader for a minor character, Segismundo Ballester, in *Fortunata y Jacinta* so that his attraction toward Fortunata will be more effective in revealing her real merit and so that his comments about her at the end of the novel will be taken seriously by the reader.

Ballester is a pharmacist who works in the same pharmacy as Maxi Rubín; his role in the novel is minor until its last few pages. Galdós elicits the reader's good will for Ballester by showing Ballester encouraging the naive, insufficiently self-reliant Ponce in his literary pursuits, and dissuading him from marrying the frivolous Olimpia Samaniego (v, 503–504). The novelist makes this clarification of Ballester's interest in Fortunata:

> Ballester era el corazón más honrado y generoso del mundo, y tenía cierta vanidad en tomar sobre sí el cumplimiento de los deberes que correspondían a otros y que estos otros olvidaban. Y aunque alentara con respecto a la señora de Rubín pretensiones amorosas a plazo largo, no dejaban por eso de ser puros y desinteresados sus actos de caridad, y habrían sido lo mismo aun en el caso de que su amiga espantara de fea y careciese de todo atractivo personal. (v, 504)

After Fortunata gives birth to her child by Juanito Santa Cruz, Ballester brings her medicine, gives her good advice, and provides her with his company (v, 526–527). In visiting Fortunata he is risking his job, since he works in the pharmacy of the Samaniegos (v, 533), whose daughter Aurora has been physically attacked by Fortunata because she has become Juanito's new mistress. Even though Ballester is dismissed from his job after Fortunata's death (v, 545), he buys roses and a tombstone for her grave (v, 546) and intends to pay for the funeral expenses, but gives in when doña Guillermina Pacheco insists that she will not allow this (v, 541–542).

Aside from practical considerations, such as providing

96

Fortunata with medicine from the pharmacy, Ballester's principal function in the novel is to reveal the attitude of the author toward Fortunata and what happened to her. Galdós gains the reader's sympathy for Ballester by making him charitable, thereby making the reader more confident of the reliability of the pharmacist's statements at the end of the novel. The gist of what Ballester says in a conversation with Maxi is that Fortunata has an angelic nature (v, 541–542). Thus he confirms her similarity to the angelic Jacinta, whom she had desired to resemble, and her authentic growth toward charitableness.

In the empathy that Maxi Rubín shows for the eccentric, deluded José Ido del Sagrario, Galdós implies that this character should elicit from the reader something more than laughter. Maxi is capable of empathy with Ido because he too has been ridiculed for acts considered by others to indicate his insanity. Galdós, then, implies that the proper attitude toward both of these men is one of compassion. Maxi defends his friend and reprimands a group of people in a cafe when they laugh at Ido for insisting, erroneously of course, that his wife is committing adultery and that he will kill her that day: "Señores, no burlarse de este pobre señor, que no tiene la cabeza buena. Un trastorno mental es el mayor de los males, y no es cristiano tomar estas cosas a broma" (v, 491).[9]

The hypocrisy of the tolerance of the marqués de Torralba, the godfather and tutor of don Carlos de Tarsis in *El caballero encantado,* is made clear in the first three chapters of the novel. The marqués's tolerance is described as a function of his laziness: "Aunque el buen señor vivía en continuo metimiento con gente de sotana y hocicaba con el marqués de Yébenes, estaba como quien dice, forrado por dentro de tolerancia y benignidad, virtudes que no eran más que formas de pereza" (vi, 223). When don Carlos asks his tutor for a loan, the marqués replies that he pities him but it would not be right to use the money which his wife left him to devote to pious ends on Carlos's cars and mistresses.[10] The marqués uses this pretext in order to refuse lending Carlos money despite the fact that he himself has had many affairs, albeit discreet ones (vi, 228).

The Plot

Plot must be conceived of in broader terms in Galdós's novels than is often the case, since, as Eoff has pointed out, characterization and plot frequently merge because the Spaniard's novels are often character studies.[11] Accordingly, what happens inside a character in the development of the novel is usually more important than the external events, which are traditionally held to constitute the plot of a novel. It must be kept in mind here that plot refers to both the external events, which forward the action of the novel, and the internal or psychological events, which also are dynamic elements of the plot.[12]

No discernible difference between the *Novelas de la primera época* and the *Novelas españolas contemporáneas,* with regard to the frequency of the appearance of charity in the plot, has been detected. However, Galdós's tendency to portray his characters more extensively and with greater "roundness" in the second group of novels has the result of making his employment of charity in the plot less obvious and consequently more effective. For example, a character in one of the *Novelas de la primera época* may be characterized with several traits more often than in the later novels. The function of the trait of charitableness is more likely to be perceived by the reader in these novels than in the later novels, where charitableness is often one among many traits ascribed to a character. It is as if Galdós found a superior caulking material in his later novels, enabling him to blend the various novelistic elements together in an apparently seamless fashion.

Galdós portrays some characters as charitable, or he has them perform an act of charity with the intention of making their subsequent participation in the plot credible to the reader. A character, for example, is described by the author as possessing the trait of kindness so that when he performs a charitable act later which contributes to the plot, the reader will find the act plausible. The attribution of kindness to the character is, of course, a part of characterization, but in the instances examined here the characterization plays a subordinate role to plot. In this section then, I reveal an aspect of Galdós's technique for integrating elements of characterization and plot.

The reader of *El audaz* (1871) is prepared for the aristocratic Susana Cerezuelo's mistreatment of Pablo Muriel. Pablo is taken into the Cerezuelo home as a servant by the conde de Cerezuelo upon the receipt of the posthumous request of the boy's father, who had died in jail as a final consequence of an unjust accusation made by the conde. Susana's unkind treatment of Pablo is one of the contributing factors in his decision to run away. Galdós prepares the reader for this event in his first description of Susana. Among several other characteristics ascribed to her is that of not loving children: "Decían que ofrecía la singularidad, inconcebible en su sexo, de no amar ni a los niños" (IV, 268).

When the conde de Cerezuelo receives the letter from Pablo's father, requesting that he take care of the boy, Galdós must make the conde charitable enough to take the boy in, but not so charitable that this trait contradicts the weak selfishness that makes him such malleable material in the hands of his nefarious overseer, Lorenzo Segarra, who was primarily responsible for the arrest of Pablo's father in the first place. The conde, who learns of the death of Pablo's father at the same time that he receives the request to take care of the boy, tells his overseer that "ya es tiempo de perdonar" (IV, 374). Galdós avoids making the conde unbelievably charitable by attributing to him a selfish motive in his decision to allow Pablo to live in his home: "No quiero abandonarle: porque ya ves, Lorenzo, su padre me sirvió, aunque mal; yo me muero mañana" (IV, 276). This apparent charitableness, then, makes possible the cruel treatment which Pablo receives in the Cerezuelo household (IV, 276–282), eventually causing him to run away. The ultimate consequence of his flight is the reunification of the revolutionary protagonist, Pablo's older brother Martín, and Susana in Toledo, where Susana proves her love for Martín by bringing the recently found Pablo to him.

Don Tomás de Albarado y Gibraleón, an official of the Inquisition, is characterized as charitable in general and affectionate in particular toward Susana, so that her plea that he use his influence to obtain the release of Leonardo, a close friend of Martín Muriel, from an inquisition jail, will not fall on deaf ears. The author says this of the doctor in canonical law: "Pero el buen teólogo era an extremo débil, sobre todo cuando se trataba de hacer bien, y Susana, que en su rara penetración lo conocía, había aprendido a sacar partido de su buen corazón" (IV, 311). The doctor is unable to do anything to secure Leonardo's release, but he is able to inform Susana that the accused man has been transferred to Toledo, where he will be tried with greater leniency.

In *Fortunata y Jacinta* when the illegitimate child which Fortunata has by Juanito Santa Cruz, Jacinta's husband, is born, doña Guillermina Pacheco, a friend of Jacinta, makes herself a guardian of the child: "Porque ha de saber usted que Dios me ha hecho tutora de este hijo. . . . Si, buena moza, no se espante no me ponga esos ojazos. Su madre es usted; pero yo tengo sobre él una parte de autoridad. Dios me la ha dado. Si su madre le faltara, yo me encargo de darle otra y tambien abuela" (v, 513). Doña Guillermina's presumptuous but well-meaning protection of the child facilitates his adoption by Jacinta when Fortunata dies later.

In *Nazarín* Estefanía (la Chanfaina), the owner of the boarding house in which the priest Nazarín stays, is characterized as charitable, so that her warning to Andara that she must leave Nazarín's quarters will be credible to the reader. Andara had been cared for by Nazarín when she sought refuge in his room after being injured in a tavern fight. La Chanfaina warns her that her whereabouts are known. The avoidance of Andara's immediate arrest makes it possible for her to accompany Nazarín later. The author prepares the reader for la Chanfaina's charitable warning by revealing that she is ill-suited to run a boarding house for poor people because she is too compassionate to insist on payment from the poor (v, 1681). She is also shown bringing food to Nazarín in his room (v, 1685). When she does warn Andara of the danger of arrest, she tells her that she does so for Nazarín's sake, to keep him from being arrested for harboring a criminal (v, 1699). Nevertheless she softens her attitude when Andara is about to leave and gives her a *peseta* (v, 1700).[13]

Although it must be kept in mind that most of the events which occur in the short novel, *La sombra* (1870), take place only in the mind of the protagonist, Anselmo, these events do constitute a plot within a plot. Anselmo relates to the narrator of the novel that he challenged to a duel the mythical Paris, who stepped out of a painting in his home to pursue his wife. Subsequently, it is learned that this hallucination is precipitated by Anselmo's extreme jealousy of his recent bride, and by the presence in his house of a handsome young man by the name of Alejandro. But the concern here is with what happens during the imagined duel. Anselmo, who inflicts on Paris what appears to be a fatal wound, is too compassionate to leave him to die alone (IV, 212); he puts him in his coach and carries him to his house only to find, to his great disappointment, that his adversary has recovered completely (IV, 212–213). Anselmo's pity, then, keeps the hallucination (and the story) from ending with a duel, since Paris continues to persecute the jealous husband.

In several cases Galdós brings characters together initially through situations involving charity. In other cases plot connections are maintained through situations involving charity. This is the case in *La Fontana de Oro* (1870) when the liberal soldier, Bozmediano, meets Clara Chacón. In a chance encounter, he defends her reactionary guardian don Elías Orejón against a group of rowdy supporters of constitutional government (IV, 23–24). Clara and Bozmediano are drawn together by mutual pity when the soldier meets Clara after having accompanied don Elías to his residence. The author describes Bozmediano's feeling toward Clara with these words: "El militar poco cuidadoso al fin de las imprecaciones del realista [don Elías], comenzó a sentir interés hacia aquella pobrecilla, que sin saber por qué, le inspiró mucha lástima desde el principio" (IV, 28). Bozmediano has compassion for Clara upon learning that she hardly ever leaves the house in which she lives, and he decides to find a pretext to return and learn more about her situation (IV, 26). Clara's pity for Bozmediano, upon seeing his injured hand, moves her to offer to wash it for him, thus affording Bozmediano the opportunity to talk with her and learn more about her (IV, 29). What he learns entices him to return.

The relationship between Clara and Bozmediano is maintained throughout *La Fontana de Oro* by a mixture of sexual attraction and pity which the soldier feels toward the girl. Both of these elements form a part of his motivation the second time that Bozmediano comes to the house where Clara lives somewhat tyrannized by don Elías. Bozmediano explains the reason for his return: "Pero después he sabido que es un tiranuelo que vive para martirizar a una pobre huérfana que se muere de melancolía encerrada aquí. No puedo ver con indiferencia que una persona tan guapa, tan amable, tan digna de ser feliz, pase la vida en poder de esta fiera" (IV, 67).

Later, when Lázaro, Clara's cousin, and Bozmediano's rival for Clara's affections, is arrested for political agitation, the soldier conceives of the idea of using his influence to obtain Lázaro's release from jail in order to win Clara's good will: "le parecía un acto que podía asegurarle la benevolencia de Clara" (IV, 95). When, in spite of this act of charity, Clara affirms her love of Lázaro to the soldier, Bozmediano resolves to continue to help the girl (IV, 122), who is living with the fanatical restrictive Porreño women. At the end of the novel, Bozmediano warns Lázaro that his life is in danger because of his political activities (IV, 185). The soldier then helps Lázaro and Clara, who has been ejected from the Porreño's house, escape from Madrid (IV, 186), thus revealing his disinterested generosity, and affecting the outcome of the plot.

Galdós himself states of *Fortunata y Jacinta* that there would be no story if Juanito Santa Cruz had not performed a certain charitable mission. That mission is a visit by Juanito of the ailing Estupiñá, a longtime friend and servant of the Santa Cruz family. Galdós makes this significant comment on Juanito's visit: "Y sale a relucir aquí la visita del *Delfín* al anciano servidor y amigo de su casa, porque si Juanito Santa Cruz no hubiera hecho aquella visita, esta historia no se habría escrito" (V, 40). The wherefore of this statement is not long in presenting itself, since Juanito sees

102

Fortunata eating a raw egg on his way up the stairs to Estupiñá's room. The conversation that Juanito initiates upon seeing such a rare sight (v, 41), is only the first step in a long relationship with Fortunata, which eventually involves many other characters in the novel.

As Gullón has accurately observed, doña Guillermina Pacheco's charity is one of the elements of union between the various worlds represented in *Fortunata y Jacinta*.[14] The concern here is with the role the charity which she habitually practices in one of Madrid's poor neighborhoods plays in helping her friend, Jacinta, arrange for the adoption of the child which she believes her husband had by Fortunata. Jacinta finally learns that the whole affair is a hoax, that Fortunata's child had died, and that the attempt to foist off another child on her is a scheme of Fortunata's uncle José Izquierdo to make money.

Jacinta learns about the child from José Ido del Sagrario, a friend of José Izquierdo. Jacinta accompanies Guillermina on one of her charitable missions to Ido's house in order to learn more about the child (v, 97). Doña Guillermina gives Ido money for food and clothing for the children, and Jacinta asks him about the child, who makes an appearance (v, 104–105). Meanwhile Jacinta has taken Ido aside and given him a duro. His having been taken aside makes him feel that the duro is given to him to spend on himself, not on his family (v, 106). With this duro, he invites his friend Izquierdo to eat a meal with him in a small restaurant. He uses this opportunity to tell Izquierdo that Jacinta wishes to see him (v, 110).

A meeting takes place shortly between Izquierdo, Jacinta, and doña Guillermina, but the focus here is on the use that Galdós makes of charity to further this particular part of the plot. Doña Guillermina's charity affords Jacinta an opportunity to learn more about the child in whom she is interested. The duro which Jacinta gives to Ido enables him in turn to be generous with Izquierdo and relay her message to him.

The inheritance which the Rubín brothers receive upon the death of their aunt, Melitona Llorente (v, 181), affects the plot of *Fortunata y Jacinta*. As a result of certain complications involved in the administering of the inheritance, the two older brothers Nicolás and Juan Pablo join their younger brother Maximiliano in doña Lupe's home, where Maxi lives (v, 181, 208–209). Nicolás, a priest, is responsible for Fortunata's entrance into Las Micaelas for a period of purification before her marriage with Maxi, and Juan Pablo remains in Madrid, where his life in various cafés is made a matter of observation.

Through the arrangements made by don Evaristo Feijoo, with whom Fortunata lives for a brief period of time, the young woman returns to live with her husband Maximiliano again. Moreover, the narration of the lives of some secondary and minor characters is advanced by Feijoo's charity.

When Feijoo makes Fortunata his mistress and companion, he promises her that if she follows his advice he will protect her even though it becomes necessary for them to separate (v, 333). This is exactly what happens soon, since Feijoo observes that his health is beginning to deteriorate rapidly, and he comes to the conclusion that his death is imminent. With Fortunata's welfare in mind, he advises her to go back to her husband Maxi, since otherwise she will have no decent means of supporting herself (v, 340). He further advises her to preserve appearances always (v, 342). To facilitate her reconciliation with Maxi, Feijoo suggests this possibility to doña Lupe and Juan Pablo, who are completely unaware that he is living with Fortunata (v, 340). Feijoo advises Fortunata to accept the domineering doña Lupe's advice and allow her to manage the household, since her aunt relishes these activities so much. At least, Fortunata can preserve her independence in other spheres (v, 342).

Feijoo, then makes arrangements with Juan Pablo for Fortunata's reconciliation with Maxi (v, 344). In addition, he gives Juan Pablo some money to repay an irksome debt. The author makes this comment on Feijoo's generosity:

Estas caridades discretas las hacía a menudo Feijoo con los amigos a quienes estimaba, favoreciéndoles sin humillarlos. Por supuesto, ya sabía él que aquello no era prestar, sino hacer limosna, quizá la más evangélica, la más acceptable a los ojos de Dios. Y no se dió el caso de que recordase la deuda a ninguna de los deudores, no aun a los que luego fueron ingratos y olvidadizos. (v, 346)

Feijoo also talks to Maxi directly about taking Fortunata back, telling him that he should forgive her: "La caridad por delante, detrás la indulgencia" (v, 351).

For Maxi's other brother, the priest Nicolás, Feijoo implores his friend Jacinto Villalonga, who is a politician, to arrange a canonry for the priest.[15]

While he is preparing Fortunata's husband and his relatives for her return, he gives the young wife herself some very effective advice. Since nothing pleases doña Lupe more than to be trusted with someone else's money, Feijoo will give Fortunata some money to hand over to her aunt to invest the day that she returns to Maxi.[16] The soundness of this advice is evident in doña Lupe's reaction when she receives the thousand duros from Fortunata to invest: "Lo más particular era que doña Lupe, por impulsos de tolerancia que habían surgido bruscamente en su espíritu, se esforzaba en suponer a aquel caudal una procedencia decente" (v, 360).

Aside from presenting a character who is extremely interesting as an individual and who easily wins the sympathy of the reader,[17] in Feijoo, Galdós has created a character whose charitableness affords him a very practical and natural means of advancing the plot of *Fortunata y Jacinta*.

In the 1893 work *Torquemada en la cruz* the seed planted in don Francisco Torquemada's mind by doña Lupe that he marry one of the Aguila sisters bursts into fruition through cultivation by Torquemada's friend don José Ruiz Donoso. Torquemada meets Donoso at the home of the Aguilas, whom the usurer visits to extend a loan. The usurer, who finds that the "lenguage de la generosidad" comes to his lips with difficulty when he intends to tell Cruz, the older sister, that he will forego the interest charges on the loan (v, 951), finally discovers the appropriate words and returns to tell the sisters of his generous intentions (v, 954). While he feels a new self being born as a result of this generous gesture, he also reveals a feeling of social inferiority in the presence of the noble ladies, evidenced by his excessive admiration of their aristocratic bearing and by his discomfort at his inability to speak correctly (v, 954).

It is as a solution to the problem of Torquemada's feelings of social inferiority that his friendship with Donoso serves an important plot function. Donoso is also a friend of the Aguila family and one of its principal benefactors (v, 955–956). Torquemada admires the urbane Donoso and resolves to imitate his social graces: "Dando mentalmente gracias a Dios por haberle deparado en el señor de Donoso el modelo social más de su gusto, don Francisco se proponía imitarle fielmente en aquella transformación de su personalidad que le pedían el cuerpo y el alma" (v, 957). The presence of such a model gives Torquemada the confidence to persist in his new friendship with the Aguilas. For his part, Donoso is aware of his ascendancy over Torquemada and loses no time in exerting an influence on him to make him more palatable to the Aguilas. On the first occasion that they meet, Donoso pointedly criticizes the rich who live in a miserly fashion (v, 959). After this first meeting, the author discloses that Torquemada's admiration for and friendship with Donoso increases rapidly. Torquemada imitates him in "hasta el modo de andar" (v, 961).

Donoso gives advice to the usurer about loans and the stock market which greatly widen his financial perspective,[18] and suggests that a man of his wealth should live in a more decent house. Torquemada protests but moves into another house before the week is out. The usurer's friend also plants the idea in his mind that he should get married, because then he would have someone to take care of him in his old age (v, 964–966).

Eventually, Donoso discreetly suggests to his friend that the Aguilas are in dire financial straits and could use his help. This induces Torquemada to pay for the cost of a lawsuit which the sisters have initiated to obtain the rights to a farm now in the hands of relatives (v, 967). Then the astute Donoso brings up the idea of Torquemada's marrying one of the sisters (v, 169). Torquemada is amenable to this idea, although Donoso's proposal leaves him perplexed as to which of the two sisters he is to marry (v, 970–971). The sisters themselves make the decision later that Fidela, the younger

of the two, will marry him, while Donoso serves as an inter-
mediary between Torquemada and them (v, 976–977). When
Torquemada is well-adjusted to the idea of marrying, Donoso
tells him that his marriage will, among other things, be a
solution to the impoverishment of the Aguilas, since he himself has become indebted as a result of his wife's illness and
can no longer help them financially (v, 975–977). After
Torquemada's marriage with Fidela, Donoso's appearance
in the novel is very rare; he has served an important function in advancing the plot of the novel and is then virtually
disposed of by the author.

In a few instances charity serves in the resolution of the
plot, in Galdós's novels. At the end of *El audaz,* the author
informs the reader that Pablillo, the younger brother of the
protagonist of the novel, Martín Muriel, has been brought up
and educated by Muriel's friend Leonardo and his wife
Engracia. Furthermore, he has been placed by this couple in
the *Seminario de Nobles.* This is in fulfillment of a suggestion
made by Susana Cerezuelo in a letter which she wrote before committing suicide (IV, 403). Much earlier, she had
mistreated Pablillo.

When the narrator and protagonist of *Lo prohibido* (1884–
1885) José María Bueno de Guzmán, not only loses most
of his fortune but also becomes almost completely paralyzed
as a result of a fall, his friend Severiano Rodríguez and
his cousin by marriage Cristóbal Medina help him salvage
what is left of his fortune (IV, 1878–1890), making it possible
for him to meet his obligation to some distant relatives who
had entrusted him with a sum of money to invest for them
(IV, 1879). The help of these two friends also makes it possible for José María to make Camila and Constantino
Miquis, who had cared for him selflessly after his fall, his
heirs (IV, 1887).

The Setting

Although the social setting is substantially established in the
first few pages of virtually all of Galdós's novels, it is by no
means exhausted there. The elaboration of the setting continues throughout the individual novels; nearly always when

a new character is introduced, Galdós gives background information on that character. Moreover, a change in the place of action is usually accompanied by a description of the new scene. Galdós's novels are organic in the sense that his novelistic creatures have roots in the past and are carefully situated in a perceptible environment in the present. In other words, the author not only presents solidly drawn characters for the reader's direct mental contemplation, but also he creates a background which fills the peripheral vision of his mind's eye, giving him thus a more irrefrangible illusion of reality.

Encarnación Guillén (la Sanguijuelera) in *La desheredada* brought up her niece and took in the latter's son Mariano, when the niece died and the boy's father was committed to an insane asylum (IV, 980). Mariano is the younger brother of Isidora Rufete, the protagonist of the novel. Isidora arrived in Madrid with sufficient money, as she puts it, "para poner a Mariano en una escuela y para vestirme con decencia" (IV, 983). The money was given to her by her uncle, don Santiago Quijano-Quijada, a quixotic canon with whom she had been living in La Mancha (IV, 983). This same relative had paid for second-class quarters for Isidora's father in the insane asylum at Leganés (IV, 973).

The events occurring prior to the action-time of *Tristana* (1892), which resulted in Tristana Reluz becoming don Lope Garrido's ward, are related early in the novel. Don Lope, who has always been willing to "dar la camisa por un amigo," found himself in the position to do so when his friend and Tristana's father Antonio went into debt and was incarcerated as a result of an unsuccessful business venture. In order to rescue his despairing friend, don Lope sold a house and a collection of pictures (V, 1544), explaining his generosity to Reluz in this manner: "El dinero no deja de ser vil sino cuando se ofrece a quien tiene la desgracia de necesitarlo. Yo no tengo hijos. Toma lo que poseo; que un pedazo de pan no ha de faltarnos" (V, 1545). Shortly after Reluz was released from jail he died, leaving a widow and his daughter Tristana, who was nineteen years old at the time. Don Lope's altruism was soon tested again when Reluz's widow contracted a fatal illness and don Lope felt constrained to pay her medical bills and the cost of the funeral. To do this he sacrificed a precious collection of arms (v, 1546). Furthermore, in fulfillment of a recommendation made by the moribund woman don Lope agreed to take care of Tristana (v, 1546-1547).

In this same novel, Galdós relates the cruelty inflicted upon Horacio, Tristana's suitor, by his grandfather, a business man:

> Pues, señor, aquel tigre cogió al pobre Horacito a los trece años, y como medida preventiva le ataba las piernas a las patas de la mesa escritorio, para que no saliese a la tienda ni se apartara del trabajo fastidioso que le imponía. Y como le sorprendiera dibujando monigotes con la pluma, los coscorrones no tenían fin. (v, 1557)

Galdós uses charity to form a part of the setting in order to characterize Orbajosa in *Doña Perfecta*. When Pepe Rey enters Orbajosa, Galdós reinforces the engineer's negative impression of the city by lining the entrance with numerous beggars: "Los repugnantes mendigos que se arrastraban a un lado y otro del camino pidiendo el óbolo del pasajero ofrecían lastimoso espectáculo" (v, 413). Later, when Pepe comments on the need for finding jobs for this "ejército lastimoso," the priest don Inocencio rejects such a solution by replying: "Para eso está la caridad" (IV, 419).

Remarks made in *Doña Perfecta* by Galdós and some of the characters about the charitableness of the people of Orbajosa, prove to be ironic in intent as the action of the novel unfolds and the reader is made to perceive the massive intolerance of the Orbajosans. Before Pepe Rey came to Orbajosa, his father had praised the goodness of its citizens in this fashion: "Allí toda es bondad, honradez; allí no se conocen la mentira y la farsa como en nuestras ciudades; allí renacen las santas inclinaciones que el bullicio de la vida moderna ahoga" (IV, 415).

The language of charity is on the lips of Tío Licurgo, when he takes leave of Pepe after having accompanied him from the railway station to doña Perfecta's house: "Dios le conserve sus días para favorecer a los pobres" (IV, 418). Tío Licurgo loses no time, however, in bringing a lawsuit against Pepe to deprive the young engineer of lands which rightfully belong to him.

Amidst these ironies, the author inserts this explicit statement on the intolerance of the Orbajosans of the *casino:* "Lo que principalmente distinguía a los orbajosenses del casino era un sentimiento de viva hostilidad hacia todo lo que fuera viniese" (IV, 438).[19]

When the antiquary, don Cayetano Polentinos, paints a millenial picture of life in Orbajosa, the reader has already been sufficiently exposed to the hypocrisy of the Orbajosans to perceive the irony involved: "Aquí todo es paz, mutuo respeto, humildad cristiana. La caridad se practica aquí como en los tiempos evangélicos; aquí no se conoce la envidia" (IV, 453).

The vein of irony with respect to the charitableness of the Orbajosans is continued when Galdós makes this comment on the rumors (unfounded of course) that are spread about the supposedly atrocious conduct of Pepe prior to his break with doña Perfecta: "Todo el mundo los [rumors] repetía, y los comentarios iban siendo tantos que si don Cayetano los recogiese y compilase, formaría con ellos un rico Thesaurum de la benevolencia orbajosense" (IV, 466).

The irony which Galdós uses in describing the charitableness of the Orbajosans has the effect of dramatizing the extent of their uncharitableness as the monolithic presence of the latter is gradually revealed.

In *Torquemada en el purgatorio* Torquemada's sister-in-law Cruz suggests that Torquemada become a senator, and the miser replies only half-humorously: "Ya estoy viendo la nube de parientes con hambre atrasada que van a caer sobre mí como la langosta" (V, 1067). Later, when Torquemada has become a senator, it is evident that he knew whereof he spoke, since in fact a horde of beggars and *cesantes* do descend upon him. He gets rid of them by giving them alms (V, 1074–1075). By having Torquemada's apparently hyperbolic prediction come true, Galdós underscores the existence of widespread poverty in Spain.

The principal function of some instances of charity in the social setting is to provide a visible means of support to a character for the purpose of maintaining the verisimilitude

110

of that character's actions. For example, a very minor character, el Doctrino in *La Fontana de Oro,* is able to pursue his political activities with a minimum of "thought for the morrow," since the executors of his father's estate give him a sum of money about every six months (iv, 50). This money is supplemented by money which his friends give to him (iv, 50–51).

The dedicated nun Leré in *Angel Guerra* has a brother to whom she refers as a "monstruo" because of his severe congenital physical defects. Leré says that her brother is cared for devotedly by her aunt Justina and uncle Roque: "Hoy le tienen y le cuidan mis tíos, que viven junto al Pozo Amargo, y no hay obra de caridad que a ésta se compare, porque otros le habrían tirado a un muladar o en mitad de un camino" (v, 1259).

The novelist employs many techniques to fuse the various elements of his novel into a creative whole which aspires to seamlessness. In Galdós's novels situations involving charity are used frequently to contribute to this synthesizing process. This phenomenon then, considered along with the importance of charity as an idea and emotion, illustrates the interrelatedness of form and substance characteristic of all good art.

Notes

1 José Balseiro, *Novelistas españoles modernos* (1933), p. 213.

2 According to Forster, "flat" characters are those who possess a single attribute or trait, whereas "round" characters reveal several "factors" for the reader's consideration and are "capable of surprising in a convincing way." There is, of course, a spectrum, ranging from "flatness" to "roundness"; see E. M. Forster, *Aspects of the Novel* (1927), pp. 67–78.

3 See also iv, 1318–1319, 1320.

4 See also iv, 1537–1540.

5 See also iv, 449.

6 While admitting the exaltation of charity in *Misericordia,* Eoff, in *The Novels of Pérez Galdós: The Concept of Life as Dynamic Process* (1954), pp. 17–23, avers that Galdós has created in Benina a character who grows notably. The evidence which he marshals for this interpretation, are the expository remarks in which the author relates Benina's humble origins and her reputation for being a "sisona," her temporary recourse to superstition, and Benina's obvious moral ascendancy over

Juliana and doña Paca, at the end of the novel. In addition, Eoff cites as evidence of this growth her ability to cope with the increasingly difficult tests of her charitableness.

[7] Orlando, "Novelas españolas del año literario," *Revista de España* 100 (1884): 431.

[8] See also v, 132–133, 314, 316, 317.

[9] W. H. Shoemaker has already pointed out the irony of Maxi's attitude toward Ido in "Galdós's literary creativity: D. José Ido del Sagrario," *HR* 19 (1951): 222–223.

[10] See also vi, 235.

[11] Eoff, *The Novels of Pérez Galdós,* p. 3.

[12] Eoff, in "The Treatment of Individual Personality in *Fortunata y Jacinta,*" p. 267, aptly calls the plot consisting of internal changes, the "psychological plot."

[13] An additional example of the role which charity plays in the preparation for plot development is found in the description which Galdós gives of the priest, don Romualdo in *Misericordia* (v, 1991, 1996). By attributing generosity to the priest, the author makes his subsequent charitableness toward Benina and Almudena more plausible.

[14] See Ricardo Gullón, "Estudio preliminar y bibliografía" to *Miau* by Benito Pérez Galdós (1957), p. 83.

[15] v, 355–356. At the same time that Feijoo pleads for a canonry in behalf of Nicolás, he also entreats Villalonga to find a job for the unemployed bureaucrat don Ramón Villaamil.

[16] v, 347. Feijoo also leaves some stocks for Fortunata in a bank; see v, 355.

[17] If the sincerity of Feijoo's charity is not clear from the statement made by the author when the former colonel lends Juan Pablo money, then it should be amply evident when the ailing Feijoo revises his will, making many beneficent dispositions, tearing up IOU notes of needy friends, and distributing his jewelry amongst his friends.

[18] v, 963. In *Torquemada en el purgatorio* (1894), the author states that Donoso had helped Torquemada surround himself with friends who could help him increase his wealth (v, 1022).

[19] See also iv, 460.

VI Conclusions

A DETAILED ANALYSIS of Galdós's novels has vindicated the numerous critics who have stressed the importance of the theme of charity or nonsexual love in the Spanish writer's works. This is true not only because of the extensive and constant presence of this theme throughout his novels but also because of the depth of treatment which he accords the theme of charity. A study of his novels has revealed a high degree of consistency in his presentation of charity. Moreover, he has been discovered to have made frequent use in his novels of situations in which the exercise of charity plays a significant part—a fact largely neglected by most of his critics—in that it is used to aid in characterization, establishing the tone, advancing the plot, and providing the setting.

While an examination of the differences which have been discerned between Galdós's presentation of charity and its opposites in the *Novelas de la primera época* and their presentation in the *Novelas españolas contemporáneas* does not reveal any fundamental changes in the novelist's attitude toward charity as he matures, there is disclosed a gradual shift in focus to the more positive aspects of the theme and a refinement in the creation of situations in which charity is prominent as a literary tool.

An analysis of the psychological aspects of charity has disclosed that hate arising from gross physical aggression is found throughout Galdós's novels, e.g., from *Doña Perfecta* to *Casandra,* but hate which has its genesis in the slow, subtle, and insidious usurpation of one's personality, as in the case of Cruz del Aguila's cannibalization of don Francisco Torquemada's soul in the last three novels of the

Torquemada series, is absent in the *Novelas de la primera época.*

With regard to the psychological principles underlying his treatment of the theme of love in the novels, Galdós has revealed considerable consistency and an astonishing working knowledge of subconscious levels of the personality. Galdós's psychology of love presupposes a conception of personality according to which each individual possesses a permanent inner self which is resistant to alien influences. This has been especially demonstrated in the respective discussions of doña Paulita Porreño in *La Fontana de Oro* and Angel Guerra, and the other abnormal characters in the novels. One of the central characteristics of the inner self which the individual shares with all other individuals is the need to love and be loved. Those characters who fail to love invariably suffer some form of psychological retribution, e.g., Juliana's guilt feelings in *Misericordia,* while those who are the objects of hatred or insufficient love either suffer greatly or are destroyed as happens to Pepe Rey in *Doña Perfecta* and Maxi Rubín in *Fortunata y Jacinta.* The principle that love begets love and hate engenders hate has been demonstrated throughout the novels.

I have observed that individuals in Galdós's novels who for various reasons attempt to repress their physical love for another or replace it with some other activity (usually religious) inevitably find that the physical love asserts itself in the end, e.g., doña Paulita Porreño in *La Fontana de Oro.* Galdós was revealed to be in agreement with some contemporary psychoanalysts who affirm that sublimation is never completely effective as a means of rechanneling sexual energy. At the same time that Galdós stresses the common need of human beings to love and be loved, he also takes into account individual differences in the ability to give of oneself to others. Thus self-abnegation comes more easily to doña Guillermina Pacheco or Leré than to Fortunata or Angel Guerra.

An examination of the sociological aspects of charity in Galdós's novels has made it clear that in an area in which there might have appeared to be many contradictions, the novelist actually exhibits a great deal of consistency. Galdós

114

avoids condemning organized charity per se. What he does condemn are those who would rely completely upon organized charity as a remedy for widespread social injustice, e.g., don Inocencio in *Doña Perfecta*. It has been demonstrated in *Marianela* and *El amigo Manso* that those who devote themselves to organized charity are usually more interested in the social satisfactions to be derived therefrom than in alleviating the misery of the poor. Galdós has been shown to deplore the attitude which permits the individual to be complacent about social injustice precisely because he contributes to organized charity, e.g., Sofía in *Marianela*. Furthermore, he reveals how reliance upon charity in Spain has created the expectation on the part of great numbers of people being able to live without working; charity when substituted for justice too often fosters mendicancy and parasitism, e.g., the Tellerías in *La familia de León Roch* and the Bringas in *Tormento* and *La de Bringas*. The implication of the portrayal of Golfín in *Marianela* is that true charity will seek to provide justice. In the activities of doña Guillermina Pacheco in *Fortunata y Jacinta* Galdós's belief that the individual who is motivated by a sincere desire to help others can alleviate misery in a small corner of the world, even if it is done through institutions, has been made manifest.

Although public beneficence was revealed to be an infrequent theme in the novels, Galdós does indicate that its administrators on the whole seem to be more concerned with public order than with individual misery. In *La desheredada* public officials spend a great sum of money on a new bull ring rather than on badly needed schools. And the general public applauds this preference.

With respect to the religious and ethical aspects of love in the early novels Galdós focuses more often on hate and destructive religious forces, e.g., *Doña Perfecta, Gloria, La familia de León Roch*. While these forces are not absent in the later novels, a greater emphasis in novels such as *Nazarín, Halma, Misericordia,* and *El abuelo* on the positive ethic of love is evident.

The study demonstrates conclusively that the characters in Galdós's novels who advocate most vociferously that it is man's duty to love God and those individuals in the novels who are the most insistent upon the necessity of observing external religious forms usually exhibit less love for their neighbors than would seem consonant with their verbal stance, e.g., doña Juana in *Casandra*. Galdós views love as an emotion rather than as a duty. It is a duty, of course, even according to the teachings of Christ, but the novelist agrees that the emphasis must be upon love as a feeling, as he makes clear in his respective portrayals of Gloria and Benina. In *Nazarín* love of man is made equivalent to love of God.

Galdós has demonstrated that he is both ancient and modern in his view of charity: ancient in that he stresses the primitive teaching of Christ on love as a feeling, and modern in that he would break the theological accretions that have accumulated on Christ's teachings on love and hardened them into dogmas. Dogma, according to Galdós's view in *Doña Perfecta, Gloria,* and *La familia de León Roch,* is a divisive influence in human affairs; the characters who hold to dogma tend to polarize human beings around clusters of ideas and find it difficult to love another person as a unique human being but rather accept or reject him according to his ideas. This is most dramatically demonstrated in doña Perfecta's destruction of her own nephew because of his supposed atheism.

While charity should be a positive element in human relations, in the conduct of Tomás Orozco in *La incógnita* and *Realidad,* it has been found to be an instrument of self-perfection, self-perfection poorly understood it should be added. Although Orozco undoubtedly does some good through his charity, he is depicted as using other people as a means to his own self-perfection. This gradually results in a self-righteousness on his part which alienates him from ordinary mortals, including his own wife.

The exaltation of love as the supreme ethical value has been revealed to be the main thrust of Galdós's efforts in *Misericordia.* Benina's all-consuming charitable activities give precedence to love over all other forms of human relationships. The novelist has presented love—not race, class, creed, or profession—as the tie that ideally should bind human beings together.

Ultimately, it must be concluded that Galdós advocates

the practice of a charity which is fundamentally religious yet humanitarian. He would be rid of the false dichotomy between man's natural needs and his physical needs created by dogmatic religion and administer to the needs of the whole man. This is true throughout his novels, but the novelist's advocacy of a charity which is humanitarian in its orientation is seen most clearly in the novels of his creative maturity.

Don Benito has been found to employ charity in three ways in characterization. In the first place, while charity nearly always appears as a factor in contributing to the complexity of his characters, giving them what E. M. Forster calls "roundness," there are some cases of love the only discernible function of which is to make a character more complex, e.g., Pedro Polo's kindness toward Celedonia in *Tormento*. Secondly, charity is used to add dramatic interest to the novels. Characters are contrasted (foils) in the trait of charitableness, e.g., Cucúrbitas and Guillén in *Miau*. Lastly, charity is used in the development of characters. For example, it has been shown in the discussion of *La desheredada* how Isidora Rufete's imperviousness to all good advice and kindness indirectly reveals her personality.

Although Galdós has several means of indicating his attitude toward a given character, the study has revealed that one of the more subtle, and therefore more effective ways in which he does this, is through attributing charitableness or uncharitableness to a character. The novelist has used this technique with a great deal of assurance of conveying his attitude to the reader because of the accuracy of his assumption that kindness is a universally admired trait, while its various opposites such as cruelty and envy are uniformly considered repugnant. It should be made clear that other factors have had to be considered in determining the tone of Galdós's novels. The attribution of charitableness to a character is one way of aiding in establishing the tone; by no means does it reveal everything about Galdós's attitude toward what he has written. The attribution of charitableness of a character is often merely one of several vectors which the reader must take into account in order to discover the attitude of the author toward that character. For example, Galdós attributes generosity to Pepa Fúcar in *La familia de León Roch* revealing at the same time her thoughtlessness by the indiscriminate manner in which she gives.

Although the examination of Galdós's novels has revealed that charity is just as essential an element in the plot of the *Novelas de la primera época* as in the *Novelas españolas contemporáneas,* there has been disclosed an increased subtlety in his use of charity in the plot in the second group of novels. Since most of the characters in the *Novelas de la primera época* are ascribed a smaller number of traits than those of the *Novelas españolas contemporáneas,* the attribution of the trait of charitableness to a character with the specific purpose of preparing the reader for the character's subsequent performance of a charitable act which affects the plot was found to be more conspicuous in the first group of novels, as in the case of Susana Cerezuelo in *El audaz;* whereas in the second group it is unobtrusively buried among several traits, as in the case of doña Guillermina's generosity when she makes herself godmother of Fortunata's baby, thus easing her participation in the transferral of the baby to Jacinta later.

Charity serves several functions in the plots of Galdós's novels. He sometimes attributes the trait of charitableness to a character to make credible a subsequent act of charity by the character which affects the plot, e.g., in *Nazarín* the kindness of la Chanfaina toward her boarders makes credible her aid of Andara later. An act of charity is frequently instrumental in establishing initial connections between characters as when one person comes to the aid of another, e.g., Bozmediano's aid of Clara Chacón's guardian in *La Fontana de Oro.* Just as common, if not more so, is the importance of charity in maintaining relations between various characters as in the case of Jacinta and José Ido del Sagrario in *Fortunata y Jacinta.* In addition, the novelist sometimes avails himself of a situation in which charity figures prominently in the resolution of the plot. A loose end is tied up in *El audaz,* for example, when the reader learns that Leonardo and his wife Engracia have become guardians of Pablillo.

In the social setting, situations involving charity are found in the description of events occurring prior to the action-time of the novel to give the reader a more complete understanding of relationships which obtain when the action of the novel begins or of conditions which are sustained during the action of the novel, e.g., the description of Encarnación Guillén's decision to rear Isidora and Mariano in *La desheredada*. In some cases charity serves the function in the setting of providing the reader a perspective against which to observe the deeds of the characters in the novel, e.g., the description of the beggars in *Doña Perfecta*. A third function charity performs in the social setting is the creation of an illusion of reality by providing certain characters with a visible means of support, e.g., el Doctrino in *La Fontana de Or*.

The study has revealed conclusively that Galdós's most frequent means of presenting the theme of charity is through dramatization of its presence or conspicuous absence. The vast majority of instances of charity discussed in the foregoing pages involve the words or deeds or the characters themselves rather than authorial commentary. Where Galdós comments he does so often as a further means of dramatizing, through irony or hyperbolic descriptions, the uncharitable words or deeds of the characters, e.g., *Doña Perfecta*.

A detailed examination of Galdós's novels has revealed, then, a multiplicity of facets from the ideological standpoint in the novelist's treatment of the theme of charity. The reader who quickly and wholeheartedly approves of the charity of Orozco, for example, cannot have taken into account all of the hints given by the author about his motivation. Likewise, the reader who concludes precipitately that Galdós condemns the charity of doña Guillermina Pacheco because he condemns organized charity in other novels disregards both doña Guillermina's sincerity and the desirable consequences of her charitable activities.

The manifold aspects of Galdós's attitude toward charity from the viewpoint of ideology have been found to be matched by its significance as an element of tone, characterization, plot, and setting. Furthermore, the ideological aspects of charity and its literary function are frequently integrated in single instances of charity. Thus at the same time that Galdós makes Pepe Cruz uncharitable in order to use him to criticize parasitism he also makes him a foil in charitableness to Victoria Moncada. The attribution of charitableness, or any of its opposites, to a character for the purpose of making a subsequent act of that character plausible demonstrates how characterization and plot merge in Galdós's novels. The ability to accomplish more than one objective with a single stroke is, after all, one of the hallmarks of artistic genius. Galdós's ability to achieve economy without sacrificing meaning in his use of charity makes it clear that he possesses one of the prime qualifications for marching in the ranks of mankind's great geniuses.

List of Galdós's Novels

La sombra (1870)
La Fontana de Oro (1866–1867)
El audaz (1871)
Doña Perfecta (1876)
Gloria (1876–1877)
Marianela (1878)
La familia de León Roch (1878)
La desheredada (1881)
El amigo Manso (1882)
El doctor Centeno (1883)
Tormento (1884)
La de Bringas (1884)
Lo prohibido (1884–1885)
Fortunata y Jacinta (1886–1887)
Miau (1888)
La incógnita (1888–1889)
Torquemada en la hoguera (1889)
Realidad (1889)
Angel Guerra (1890–1891)
Tristana (1892)
La loca de la casa (1892)
Torquemada en la cruz (1893)
Torquemada en el purgatorio (1894)
Torquemada y San Pedro (1895)
Nazarín (1895)
Halma (1895)
Misericordia (1897)
El abuelo (1897)
Casandra (1905)
El caballero encantado (1909)
La razón de la sinrazón (1915)

Bibliography

Alas, Leopoldo [Clarín]. Review of *Realidad, Novela en cinco jornadas* by Benito Pérez Galdós. *La España Moderna,* 13 (1890): 216–223.

———. *Galdós.* Madrid: Renacimiento, 1912.

Angeles, José. "Baroja y Galdós: Un ensayo de diferenciación," *Revista de Literatura,* 23 (1963): 45–46.

———. "¿Galdós precursor del noventa y ocho?" *Hispania,* 46 (1963): 265–273.

Aranguren, José Luis L. *Etica.* Madrid: Revista de Occidente, 1958.

Balseiro, José A. *Novelistas españoles modernos.* New York: Las Americas, 1963.

Barja, César. *Libros y autores modernos.* Los Angeles: Campbell's Book Store, 1933.

"Beneficencia," *Enciclopedia Universal Ilustrado.* Vol. 11.

Berkowitz, H. C. Introduction to *El abuelo: Drama en cinco actos* by Pérez Galdós. New York: D. Appleton Century, 1929.

———. *Pérez Galdós: The Spanish Liberal Crusader.* Madison: University of Wisconsin Press, 1948.

Brooks, J. L. "The Character of Doña Guillermina Pacheco in Galdós' Novel *Fortunata y Jacinta,*" *BHS,* 38 (1961): 87–94.

Casalduero, Joaquín. "Ana Karenina y Realidad," *Bulletin Hispanique,* 39 (1937): 375–396.

———. *Vida y obra de Galdós.* 2nd ed. Madrid: Gredos, 1961.

Cejador y Frauca, Julio R. *Historia de la literatura castellana.* Vol. 2. Madrid: Revista de Archivos, 1918.

Clarke, Gerard Roy. "The Christian Ideal in Selected Novels of Benito Pérez Galdós." Diss., University of Pennsylvania, 1968.

Correa, Gustavo. *El simbolismo religioso en las novelas de Pérez Galdós.* Madrid: Gredos, 1962.

Dickens, Charles. *Bleak House.* Vol. 1. Cambridge: Riverside, 1869.

Drever, James. *A Dictionary of Psychology.* London: Hazell Watson and Viney, 1955.

122

Eoff, Sherman. *The Novels of Pérez Galdós: The Concept of Life as Dynamic Process.* St. Louis: Washington University Press, 1954.

_____. *The Modern Novel.* New York: New York University Press, 1961.

Forster, E. M. *Aspects of the Novel.* New York: Harcourt, Brace and World, 1927.

Fromm, Erich. *The Art of Loving.* New York: Harper and Row, 1956.

Gamero, y de Laiglesia, Emilio. *Galdós y su obra.* Vol. 2. Madrid: Ruiz, 1934.

Gramberg, J. Edward. *Fondo y forma del humorismo de Leopoldo Alas, "Clarín,"* Oviedo: Gráficas Summa, 1958.

Gullón, Ricardo. "Estudio preliminar y bibliografía" to *Miau* by Benito Pérez Galdós. Madrid: Revista de Occidente, 1957.

Hafter, Monroe Z. "Ironic Reprise in Galdós' Novels," *PMLA,* 76 (1961): 233-239.

Hall, Calvin S. *A Primer of Freudian Psychology.* New York: New American Library, 1955.

Hume, Martin. *Modern Spain.* 3rd. ed. London: Carey, 1923.

Hüsges, Hubert. *Der Schriftseller Benito Pérez Galdós (1843-1920) als Vorkämpfer des Liberalismus in Spanien.* Borna-Leipzig: Universitätsverlag von Robert Noske, 1928.

Iwanik, John. "A Study of the Abnormal Characters in the Novels of Benito Pérez Galdós." Diss., Cornell University, 1949.

Jobit, Pierce. *Les educateurs de L'Espagne contemporaine.* Paris: Boccard, 1936.

Keniston, Hayward. "Galdós, Interpreter of Life," *Hispania,* 3 (1920): 203-206.

Kercheville, F. M. "Galdós and the New Humanism," *MLS,* 16 (1931): 477-489.

_____, and Eliot, L. W. "Galdós and Abnormal Psychology," *Hispania,* 23 (1940): 23-36.

Langer, Susanne. *Philosophy in a New Key: A Study in the Symbolism of Reason, Rite, and Art.* New York: New American Library, 1956.

López Morillas, Juan. *El Krausismo español.* Mexico City: Fondo de Cultura Económica, 1956.

Madariaga, Salvador de. *The Genius of Spain.* Oxford: Oxford University Press, 1923.

Menéndez y Pelayo, Marcelino. "Don Benito Pérez Galdós," *Estudios de crítica literaria.* Madrid: Revista de Archivos, 1908. Speech read in 1897 on the occasion of Galdós's entrance into the *Real Academia Española.*

Onís, Federico de. *Ensayos sobre el sentido de la cultura española.* Madrid: Publicaciones de la Residencia de Estudiantes, 1932.

Ortega y Gasset, José. *Ideas y creencias.* 8th ed. Madrid: Revista de Occidente, 1959.

Paolini, Gilberto. *An Aspect of Spiritualistic Naturalism in the Novels of B. P. Galdós: Charity.* New York: Las Americas, 1969.

Pérez de Ayala, Ramón. *Divagaciones literarias.* Madrid: Mercadal, 1958.

Pérez Galdós, Benito. *Obras completas.* Ed. F. C. Sainz de Robles. Madrid: Aguilar, Vol. 1, 8th ed., 1964; Vol. 2, 3rd ed., 1954; Vol. 5, 3rd ed., 1961; Vol. 6, 2nd ed., 1961.

Ramos-Oliverira, Antonio. *Historia de España.* Vol. 2. Mexico: Compañía General de Ediciones, 1952.

Regalado García, Antonio. *Benito Pérez Galdós y la novela histórica española.* Madrid: Insula, 1966.

Río, Angel del. "Aspectos del pensamiento moral de Galdós," *Cuadernos Americanos,* 12 (1943): 147–168.

———. *Estudios galdosianos.* Zaragoza: Librería General, 1953.

Ross, Edward Alsworth. "Philanthropy from the Viewpoint of the Sociologist," *Intelligent Philanthropy.* Ellsworth Raris et al. Chicago: University of Chicago Press, 1930.

Royo Marín, Antonio. *Teología de la caridad.* Madrid: Autores Cristianos, 1960.

Ruiz Ramón, Francisco. *Tres personajes galdosianos: Ensayo de aproximación a un mundo religioso y moral.* Madrid: Revista de Occidente, 1964.

Russell, Bertrand. *Human Society in Ethics and Politics.* New York: Simon and Schuster, 1955.

———. *A History of Western Philosophy.* New York: Simon and Schuster, 1969.

———. *Religion and Science.* New York: Oxford University Press, 1961.

Sáenz, Hilario. "Vision galdosiana de la religiosidad de los españoles," *Hispania,* 20 (1937): 235–242.

Scatori, Stephen. *La idea religiosa en la obra de Benito Pérez Galdós.* Toulouse: Bibliothèque Franco-Americaine, 1926.

Schraibman, Joseph. *Dreams in the Novels of Galdós.* New York: Hispanic Institute, 1960.

Shoemaker, W. H. "Preliminary Study" to *Crónica de la quincena* by Benito Pérez Galdós. Princeton: Princeton University Press, 1948.

———. "Galdós' Literary Creativity: D. José Ido Del Sagrario," *HR,* 19 (1951): 204–237.

———. "Cara y cruz de la novelística galdosiana," *Hispanic Studies in Honor of Nicholson B. Adams.* Chapel Hill: University of North Carolina Press, 1966, pp. 151–166.

Sidgwick, Henry. *Outlines of the History of Ethics.* Boston: Beacon, 1964.

Sisto, David T. "Pérez Galdós' *Doña Perfecta* and Louis Bromfield's *A Good Woman,*" *Symposium,* 11 (1957): 273–280.

Steele, C. W. "The Krausist Educator as Depicted by Galdós," *KFLQ,* 5 (1958): 136–142.

Torres Bodet, Jaime. *Tres inventores de la realidad: Stendhal, Dostoyevski, Pérez Galdós.* Mexico City: Imprenta Universitaria, 1955.

Unamuno, Miguel de. *Del Sentimiento trágico de la vida.* Mexico: Azteca, 1961.

United States Foreign Commerce Bureau. "Vagrancy and Public Charities in Foreign Countries," Special Consular Reports, 9, Washington, D.C. (1893): 247–269.

Walton, L. B. *Pérez Galdós and the Spanish Novel of the Nineteenth Century.* New York: Dutton, 1927.

Weber, Robert J. *The Miau Manuscript of Benito Pérez Galdós: A Critical Study.* Berkeley: University of California Press, 1964.

Wines, Fred Howard. "Sociology and Philanthropy," *Annals of the American Academy of Political and Social Science,* 12 (1898): 49–57.

Yáñez, Agustín. "Traza de la novela galdosiana," *Cuadernos Americanos,* 11 (1943): 222–240.

Zambrano, María. *"Misericordia," Hora de España,* 11 (1938): 29–52.

Index

Miquis, Constantino, 29–30
Misericordia, 49–50, 78–87, 93, 114, 115, 116
Moncada, Victoria, 30–32, 107
Moreno, Trujillo, Carlos, 80, 82–83
Morton, Daniel, 50–51, 54–58
Muñoz y Nones, 40–41
Muriel, Martín, 23–24, 99–100
Muriel, Pablo, 99

Nazarín, 67–71
Nazarín, 49, 67–70, 100–101, 115, 116, 118
Nela, 33–36
Neo-Catholics, ix–x
Nietzsche, Friedrich, 46–47n

Onís, Federico de, xiiin
Orejón, Elías, 100–101
Orejón, Lázaro, 3
Orlando, 112n
Orozco, Tomás, 71–76, 87

Paca, doña, 79–87
Paoletti, 58, 60
Paolini, Gilberto, xiiin
Pérez de Ayala, xiiin
Pérez, Galdós, Benito: list of novels, 121
Perfecta, doña, 4–5, 91
Pez, Manuel, 28
Polo, Pedro, 89–90
Ponte, Frasquito, 80–81, 84–85
Porreño, doña Paulita, 2, 3, 9–10, 114

Quijano–Quijada, Santiago, 108

Ramos–Oliveira, Antonio, ix
Realidad, 71–76, 116
Regalado, Gracía, Antonio, 76n
Rey, Pepe, 4–5, 53–54, 91
Rio, Angel del, xii, 76n, 77n, 87n
Roch, León, 25–26, 58–60, 94–95
Rodríguez, Severiano, 107
Roma, Tía, 63
Romero, Silvestre, 50, 55
Romualdo, don, 85, 86
Rosario, 4–5, 53–54
Rosaura, 61
Rubín, Juan Pablo, 95–96, 104
Rubín, Maximiliano, 2, 5–6, 75, 97, 104
Rubín, Nicolás, 17–18, 40, 104
Rufete, Isadora, 92–93

129